Inspired
Mama

*The Empowered Mother's Guide
to an Intentional Life*

Sez Kristiansen

TCK PUBLISHING.CO

ISBN: 978-1-63161-078-3

Sign up for Sez Kristiansen's newsletter at
www.sezkristiansen.com/free

Published by TCK Publishing
www.TCKpublishing.com

Get discounts and special deals on our best selling books at
www.TCKpublishing.com/bookdeals

Check out additional discounts for bulk orders at
www.TCKpublishing.com/bulk-book-orders

This book is dedicated to Mads, Mathias, and Siska.

A woman on her way to freedom is only as strong as her roots and her wings.

The fabric of me
is mother,
the weft and warp,
woman.
Loosely woven
I am free.

CONTENTS

INTRODUCTION
The Discovery

*A journey of a thousand miles
begins with a single step.*

—*Lao Tzu*

As I LAY IN THE fetal position on my son's bunk bed, I looked up at the slats above me and felt a strange affinity to them; broken, splintered, and haphazardly taped back together. I had been in this position for a few hours, my mind racing, drowning in an exhausted abyss of mental projections, anxieties, and fears. A persistent panic filled every breath. I didn't exactly know what this experience was, but I feared I might not make it out with my sanity intact. At a certain point, I was not me anymore. I had melted into a liquid storm of mental suffering—and I had no life raft.

Hours earlier, my husband had hopelessly packed up our son and left for his parents' house, leaving me to battle it out, not knowing exactly what "it" was. I was grateful for the peace and yet petrified to be left alone with a crippling panic attack, exhaustion, and what felt like a psychotic episode. I fell headfirst into negative, horrifying, and self-destructive thoughts. *This is it*, I thought. *I'm losing my mind.*

My firstborn was a challenging sleeper, and at this point I had not slept more than two consecutive hours for nearly a year. I had also just moved to a new country and started a new job at a cutthroat fashion company. I felt a constrictive hand wrap around my soul, squeezing the very essence of my freedom from its core. This hopeless submergence was like nothing I had ever felt before. Every time I closed my eyes in an attempt to find relief, all I saw were starlit shadowy trails inside my eyelids. Asleep but awake, I was unable to rest or break the consciousness of my own anatomy. *It's no wonder sleep deprivation is a torture technique*, I thought.

$$\wp\!\!)\!\!(\!\!\wr$$

I drifted back and forth through past experiences: countries I had visited, places I had once called home, and people I sorely missed. I longed for family, familiarity, a face that might ground me in this moment of isolation. I wandered the forgotten planes of my psyche to where my childhood played, barefoot and free. I recalled the wholeness of my young life, surrounded by siblings, immersed in the joy of discovery among the bushlands of our isolated farm in South Africa. Unearthing *chongololos* (millipedes) along a dirt road lined with jacaranda trees. Spinning silk webs with the worms that nestled among the mulberry bushes. Picking delicate, yet heavily scented jasmine flowers and sucking the dew from their stems while flicking "helicopter" seeds from the top of our tree house. Bullfrogs and fireflies emerging from dusk's luminous veil. Dancing barefoot around *braais*, the fire pits that our parents lit every evening.

Our classrooms were the bush and the farm. We learned how fragile life is, how simply death comes. We learned the importance of companionship from the dogs that were always by our sides; one even saved my brother from a *rinkhals*, a venomous snake. We learned compassion and detachment from caring for lost animals, like the donkey that wandered onto our farm one day and, after being fed and watered, vanished as mysteriously as she had appeared.

More than anything, I missed the vastness of the untamed wilderness that embodied my childhood. Although we moved to different parts of South Africa, we were always close to its expansive beaches, cloud-covered mountains, and vibrant culture that bathed the land in color and song. This memory of freedom is something that has never left me; my quest to rediscover it inspired a lifelong journey to the very fringes of the world.

$\mathcal{SOCR}$

I discovered, however, that one cannot recapture an element that is inherently boundless and transient. As a young adult, I returned to South Africa after five years of living in the United Kingdom to revisit the places where I had grown up. They had morphed into unrecognizable landscapes of bricks and mortar. Acres of wilderness had been heartlessly bulldozed and replaced with commercial complexes. Violent neighborhoods had sprouted from the seeds of political despair. I realized I had lost a fundamental part of myself. Although it lived on in my childhood memories, freedom was locked in the landscape of the past.

As soon as I finished high school I went on a pilgrimage of travel and wilderness wandering. For over ten years I lived in pockets of the world where a day's work would give me room and board and I could continue to pursue the abundant liberty I once enjoyed.

I never caught up with my elusive freedom, although I once tasted her salty skin off an island in the South Pacific. I once caught her sweet scent on a passing breeze over a mountain, brushed with wild lavender. I heard notes of her thunderous heart beating from a distant desert. I felt the droplets of her tears on an ancient cobbled street corner, where soul-filled music strummed at the very chords of my soul. I was so close …

Slowly, the inner calling turned outward, numbed by external attachments and addictive vices. I found quick highs followed by insufferable lows. My lack of stability and disconnect from my intuition led to poor life choices and even more devastating soul choices. I thought that my nomadic lifestyle had given me the wings of freedom, but my roots were being eaten away by avoidance, mindlessness, and destructive habits.

Once, when I was at perhaps the most lost stage of my life, I was in Sri Lanka after a long day of hiking. I had spent years deepening my spiritual practice in the country, visiting nuns in hidden jungle temples and practicing meditation and yoga with some of Hindu's most obscure yogis. On this particular pilgrimage, I ventured out to the ancient, rocky plateau of Sigiriya, a former monastery and royal residence that dates from the third century BC. After climbing a thousand steps to reach the Lion Rock fortress, I gazed across the lush planes below, laced with pagodas and a patchwork of rice farms. Despite the earthly and spiritual beauty all around me, I was numb. *I feel so small, so detached, so lost, even amid such splendor*, I thought. I know now that this kind of emotional detachment is a symptom of true hopelessness and the antithesis of the freedom I sought.

Sri Lanka was the last nomadic life I knew before I married my husband. I moved to Denmark, learned the language, became a parent, and began an unpaid internship at a fast-paced fashion company. The little freedom I had remaining vanished rapidly into the distance.

ॐ

On this late October night, my demons finally found me. I sank into a strange mix of turmoil and exhaustion. I couldn't shake my disappointment with myself for not being truly present during all the years I spent traveling the world with freedom in my sails. I didn't even know who I was anymore. How could I possibly be a good mother?

Suddenly, something divine came through the unimaginable darkness, and a question ascended through the battlefield of mental warfare. It said, "If you believe you are going to lose your mind, then you will. So why don't you believe something else?" As I held on to this thought, this *kōan*[1], like a metaphorical life vest, I came to understand that I was ultimately in control of this unraveling situation. I could either go over the edge or I could pull myself back out. It just depended on which voice I listened to. I instinctively pulled my palms toward each other in a "prayer pose" and fell asleep for a stone-cold, uninterrupted ten hours.

Upon waking the next afternoon, my mind had softened into a quiet calm, but a question continued to reverberate deep within me: "If you don't want to be a slave to your negative thoughts, then why don't you become free of them?"

When my husband returned later that day, he opened the door and smiled nervously, uncertain of what he might find. The first words I spoke came out as a surprise, even to me. I held on to him and pleaded, "Show me how to run." For whatever reason, in that moment, I remembered the joy and energy that running gave him, and how it could transform his mood.

---

[1] In Zen Buddhism, a paradoxical question for meditation

I never had any intention of running for exercise, being fit, or shoehorning myself into Lycra. I judged those who ran as people of extremes, who liked pain, or who had nothing better to do. When I saw mothers running with their babies in strollers I would gasp at their lack of creativity. I convinced myself that I would never be "that kind of person," sacrificing the few moments I had alone to sweating it out in public. But hey, if I was a professional "runner away-er," maybe this was something I could do. Freedom and running seemed quite obvious synonyms all of a sudden.

That weekend my husband and son went with me to buy my first pair of running shoes and some winter running tights. As I walked out the door into a cold Scandinavian night, the soft moonlight sparked a snakelike shimmer down my reflective vest. I took a deep breath and whispered to myself, "Run, Sez. Run."

$$\wp\!)\!\wp$$

I was born on a peach farm in South Africa in the mid-1980s. I come from two generations of displaced people who all landed in southern Africa during the World Wars and married people from other cultures. My father was born in Zambia and my mother, Zimbabwe. They met at Victoria Falls in the 1970s. Their familial customs were a hodgepodge of Polish, Dutch, British, Scottish, and a variety of nuances they picked up from living in Africa. It was an incredible and rootless childhood; we moved across landscapes and countries according to my father's ambition to offer us more opportunity in life.

I am partly defined by my name because of how it came to be. My mother comes from a long and beautiful line of women with names that double as tongue twisters: Her name is Tania Tamara Denusia Genevieve and my *babcia's*, grandmother's, Regina Genowefa. In this tradition, she wanted to name me Sezina Tameryn, and told this to my father as he drove to the registry office on the outskirts of Johannesburg. Needless to say, my father didn't remember the name or how to spell it and ended up writing Sarah-Jayne on my birth certificate. My mother was horrified and declared that she would call me Sez in defiance of the British version my father had made up.

I was a very sensitive child and I deeply internalized the social injustices I witnessed. I also had the somewhat incongruous quality of being fiercely independent. I took my sense of displacement to the bush or the flowers or the wandering cat, would he listen, and channeled my confused emotions into poetry and journal entries.

Over the years, I came to see that home wasn't a place, but rather the two siblings and two parents I traveled with. Belonging was never something that was tied to a single culture, but to many interlacing ones, and I liked that I could somehow take what I liked from them and leave what I didn't. I never felt South African, only that I belonged to its nature, its rolling coastlines swept with hot sand dunes and lush mountain ranges.

During my several years living in northern England, I completed my final years of school. I was a very undisciplined student and did not take well to instructions. In fact, my last few years of school were spent attending classes that I didn't even have the grades for but found fascinating. I got through an entire year of psychology without having the required mathematics grades; when it came time for the final examinations, my teacher found out about my deviance and decided I had the makings of a real anarchist. He let me take the exams, and I received one of the highest grades. My English language and literature classes were for highly committed students with academic minds, neither of which described me. The Board of English Educators came into my school to tell me I would be thrown out of the class unless I created a literary masterpiece. I converted a section of *The Power of One* by Bryce Courtenay into a poem, which was printed in a national magazine and won a literary award in the UK. My whole life has followed this routine of deviance and then defiance.

As a young adult, I spent several years traveling independently. I visited some of the most remote parts of the world and spent several years in Asia and the South Pacific. I worked in textiles and marketing to fund my travels because those were the jobs that fit my university degree. But I was funneled into the only jobs available, which were for consumer fashion and lifestyle brands, rather than the jobs I truly wanted, like designing technical wear for sports brands.

My siblings and parents moved to different parts of the world, so I never had a *home* to go back to. I drifted, coasted, anchored, and then drifted again. I lived in Barcelona for a while, and then in Bangkok. I moved to Sydney for a few years and then spent some time in Samoa. I traveled back to Africa hoping to find some feeling of belonging, but then decided I was more European.

It was on a particular journey to Australia that I came across one thing worth prolonged anchoring for, and it came in the form of a Danish Viking named Mads. I met my husband in a small hostel off the northeast coast of Queensland, and for two years we had a long-distance relationship. He was in his final years of studying and I had just decided to start my own textile business in Thailand. We would meet up every few months in a different city and explore both the culture and each other. It was incredible to get to know someone through long emails and letters rather than at bars and nightclubs. After a while, the relationship reached a point where it no longer felt comfortable to be apart all the time—but since neither of us had the ability to abandon our commitments, we ended it.

In many ways, Mads was my first ever intentional manifestation because I just *knew* we were going to end up together. At the time, I had absolutely no means of making that a reality, but I woke up every day feeling certain that this person was meant to be in my life forever. We had cut off communication entirely, but I often visualized creating a unique life together, having children with him, and growing old together in love and laughter. I knew in my bones that it was meant to be, and yet saw no proof. I heard through friends that he had a Danish girlfriend, yet I still knew that he was going to be part of my life. Six months later, there was a knock on my door, and a boy with tousled blonde hair, a backpack over one shoulder, and a one-way ticket asked if he could come in.

We moved to Sri Lanka shortly after and spent a year together before getting married. It was a magnificent time to explore a country that had just been liberated from thirty years of civil war. It was largely unexplored, with many places having never seen tourists, and for a while, it felt like the kingdom was ours. We spent time in monastic villiages and hiked mountains in the early hours just to see the first lick of sunrise over the horizon. I taught English in remote towns and worked for a charity that helped give street dogs better lives through medical care and adoption.

We were married in an old Danish castle in my husband's hometown and took a trip back to South Africa to celebrate. I showed him my childhood homes, where I had spent holidays on the Garden Route, and I soon became pregnant with our first child. We came to a crossroads about where we wanted to live with a child; as much as we loved Sri Lanka, we had no family there to help and it suddenly became a priority to decide on a more concrete future. I had never thought of my future, and I even prided myself on never knowing where I was going to be from year to year, so this was the first time I'd had to seriously consider where I was going to live—and for the sake of another human being.

We moved to Denmark in 2012, arriving just in time for the birth of my son. It was a cold country with a heavily ingrained culture and incomprehensible language, but at least I had help and security, which suddenly mattered a whole lot more to me. As I was coming to grips with motherhood, I also took Danish classes and searched for a job. "The Danish Way" was a term used on a daily basis by both my husband and my in-laws, and I soon came to understand that to live here sucessfully meant becoming as Danish as possible. It was a period during which I lost a piece of who I was for the love of a child, but if not for this period of turmoil, I would never have found the strength to own and honor everything that makes me a unique, free-spirited, and truly unconventional mother.

Although my journey may be different than yours, we share more in common than we do in contrast. This is what growing up in a land of separateness has taught me and what I intend to advocate for for the rest of my life: the oneness of all people. We tend to only focus on the few differences that separate us, but there is a world of similarity in our desires, our dreams, and our struggles.

I wrote this book to help you rediscover your intuitive free spirit that empowers you to realize that your life can be lived *your* way and designed by *your own* desires through intention and aligned manifestation. I want to help you unfold your own wings, one feather at a time.

ℰℭ

Take a moment and think about what it's like to live without freedom. You never have enough time to do what you love. You never have enough energy. You lack harmony and balance and are not aligned with who you are and what you want. You experience a feeling of loss and the frustration that comes with it. Perhaps you work at a job that doesn't support your needs. You long to be more creative, more responsible for your means of income, free to choose your hours and pay.

Now think about what it's like to live without adventure. Life is monotonous. Your dreams become escape routes. You fear change, so you stay in your comfort zone, even though you may never find your purpose or be truly fulfilled. You miss out on opportunities because you fear they may harm your family. You ignore your inner voice that keeps asking if there isn't something more.

But that's not all: You worry that you're not living up to your family's or society's expectations. You don't know how to balance your own desires with your responsibilities as a wife and mother. You fear that your dreams may never become reality. Perhaps you believe that this is just the way life is, or that freedom is a privilege only for the smart or wealthy. These fears and perceptions are constrictive; they can damage your relationships, affect your children, and limit your ability to live a conscious, abundant life. They provide no space for creativity, no grounding for your roots.

This book is written in three parts, each a fundamental step toward a potent, intentional, and unconventional life. It will guide you toward conscious choices in every aspect of your life—from freeing your mind, body, and soul to freeing your life through intentional realignment and high-vibrational living. I'll share my stories to remind you that we all go through similar experiences. This connects us in a sisterhood that has the power to heal even our deepest wounds. This knowledge in itself is truly redeeming.

There are "red threads," or themes, in this book that incorporate metaphysical theories, universal laws, and reconditioning psychology. Unlike most self-empowerment theories, however, this book is written with an equal balance of feminine energy. We need our "active," risk-taking masculine energy to start creating an intentional life, but we must also connect to our "allowing" feminine nature, which makes us compassionate, nurturing, and receptive to how we *feel* about our life.

Without this balance, we strive constantly for equilibrium. If we ignore the feminine as we pursue the life of our dreams, we must often go to extremes to rebalance it. This is why some women become entirely submissive in a relationship or subdue themselves in domesticity. Balance is an art form, as every mother knows, but it is much easier to negotiate when there is a consistency between the two energies of male action and feminine allowing.

Throughout this book, I talk about the process of "intentional manifestation" as a key to freedom. The law of attraction states that your vibrations (thoughts, emotions, and behaviors) lead to patterns (habits and beliefs) that manifest (create into existence) your life experience. Your life right now is the physical manifestation of these repeated thoughts, patterns, and habits.

According to Dr. Joe Dispenza, neuroscientist, your belief patterns are deeply embedded in your subconscious mind, which controls 98 percent of your everyday activities. When you want to make changes in your life, you must shift your mindset from one of austerity on autopilot to one that thrives in conscious awareness. By making this shift, you retrain your negative habits, beliefs, and thought patterns, and make awareness the keystone of your conscious life.

This is a book for mothers who want to get stuff done *and* create an intentional life. It is practical, accessible, and filled with an awareness of the feminine energy that rules a busy mother's life.

I am in awe of you and your journey. You may not be aware of the incremental effect your self-empowerment efforts will have, but even a grain of rice can tip the scale in a collective mind-shift. By choosing freedom, intention, and adventure, you can redesign your life in accordance with your own blueprint. You will also create a new paradigm that your children can use in their own lives and pass down a worthy inheritence.

This way to freedom, Mama.

PART ONE

FREEDOM OF MIND

CHAPTER 1
Your Consciousness

*Man cannot discover new oceans unless they have
the courage to lose sight of the shore.*

—André Gide

I STARTED RUNNING IN 2013, one year after my son was born. For me, this was the seed of conscious freedom that planted itself in the folds of my soul. I suddenly became very aware that I was not limited to the small world I had created for myself. Running became a brief act of escape, which only made me run faster toward home again.

To this day I am a terrible runner. I am not very fast, and I have yet to take on a marathon. But none of that matters, because I am doing something I once believed impossible.

The simple realization that I could override what my mind told me became a stepping-stone to the world of perpetual consciousness. Before I knew it, I was skinny-dipping in the icy waters of the Kattegat, sitting in Scandinavian sweat tents, attending cacao ceremonies, and saying "hi" to total strangers, all while navigating the cultural minefield of Denmark.

Once I started to feel freer, lighter, and in control, everything became possible. I realized my rigid comfort zone and expectations had formed an impenetrable barrier that never allowed for true growth. What I once thought was a place of safety and identity actually restricted any possibility for personal empowerment.

If you're like most women, practicalities outweigh desires in the immediate changes that come with motherhood. I have yet to meet any woman, career-driven or soul-guided, who does not find it difficult to balance motherhood and personal desires. You constantly struggle to compensate for your job, lack of time, depleted energy, physical stress, financial strains, or the loss of long-held dreams. It is so normal to feel some form of discontent that many find themselves constantly out of sync. When bills need to be paid, responsibility trumps fun and your creative nature retreats to the lost playgrounds of your psyche.

Paradoxically, motherhood also makes you hearty, strong, and resilient. It gives you uncountable ways to love another soul and immeasurable compassion for the world around you. It reminds you of your connection to the past and your primal sense of purpose. You realize the fragility of life and feel depths of gratitude. It is like an intensive boot camp and spiritual retreat all in one existential experience.

My first child raised me; my second child freed me. Without them, I would have stayed in my restrictive and unconscious comfort zone where nothing grows deep, nothing is nurtured, and light never reaches the dormant seeds of true happiness. When you are dissatisfied with life, you can either fight or flee. But the worst thing you can do is nothing. As you will discover, the vibrational energy of "inspired action" plays a large role in the quest for freedom and is key to the materialization of your dreams.

In Part One, you'll find practical, incremental steps to awaken consciousness and sow the seeds of intentional freedom. In this process of discovery and alignment, you will take the lead as a conscious creator. You will be able to create meaningful space in your life by clearing out negative, repressing, and emotionally draining clutter. This section is all about letting your mental freedom flow, your imaginative energy bubble up, and your playful nature emerge.

CHAPTER 2
Your Wisdom

You are what you do, not what you say you'll do.

—*Carl Jung*

Wisdom means not only having knowledge, but being able to act on that knowledge. It's a vital tool in self-discovery. The following story outlines the external and internal tools needed for wisdom.

Two women sit in a hospital waiting room. One was a heavy smoker for twenty years but recently quit. The other woman still smokes, although she has tried to quit many times. Even though it has caused her and the people she loves enormous pain, she still finds it hard to give up the habit. A doctor walks in and asks both women if they know that smoking causes cancer, heart disease, and other serious illnesses. Both answer, "Yes."

Both women know the dangers. This is knowledge. The doctor asks the woman who no longer smokes what she did to stop smoking. She answers, "I stopped putting the cigarette in my mouth." This is action.

If you have knowledge but fail to act, you can never be the true creator of your own life. If you act without knowledge, you will be stuck in repetitive cycles of thoughts, emotions, and consequences. To break free of negative habits, you must look deeply at both knowledge and action and identify which is lacking.

There are myriad reasons why the smoker found it difficult to quit, and they apply to all of us. Culture, childhood experiences, habitual stress responses, environment, friends—these condition us not to act, even when we know we should for our families or ourselves. If we are to be conscious creators of our lives, however, knowledge combined with action (wisdom) will give us the freedom we need to live an untethered life, open to the currents and tides of transformation.

While wisdom is the door and the lock, intuition is the key that allows you to access your internal guidance. This is fundamental to living in accordance with your true self. You might know why your mind is wired a certain way, and you might even create new positive habits, but without intuition, you will ignore your internal compass and be guided instead by external expectations.

When women become mothers, intuition can become an internal navigation system. Unfortunately, the lack of inherited knowledge and regular practice seems to have dismantled this valuable tool, having been replaced by search engines. It is imperative that you relearn these innate skills, not only for yourself, but so you may gift them to your children. These intuitive skills are reinitiated in the Inspired Action, which we'll discuss towards the end of this chapter.

Let's begin by discovering the patterns that turn the wheel of your habitual life and question who you really are. With this, you gather the tools of knowledge and inspired action that empower you to become the conscious creator of your own life.

CHAPTER 3

Your Manifestation Cycle

The state of your life is nothing more than a reflection of the state of your mind.

—*Wayne W. Dyer*

YOUR DAYS ARE FILLED WITH habitual cycles: habitual thoughts, unconscious emotions, and reactive actions. It's like a wheel in continuous motion, creating and recreating your life experience. Some people have negative cycles turned by thoughts, emotions, and actions that produce even more negativity. Others' lives are full of positive thoughts, emotions, and actions. Most of us move between negative and positive themes, but one usually dominates, driven by our unconscious habits.

Your cycles, from initial emotions to actual manifestation, are the blueprint on which your entire existence is built, based on your own unique conditioning and experiences. As your life and environment become more and more habitual, your body produces predictable emotional responses to your predictable daily life. So, if you usually get stressed in morning traffic, that emotional response produces physical symptoms every time you're in morning traffic: faster pulse, shortened breath, and perspiration. Your emotions can become so attuned to this predictability that they produce the symptoms and stress hormones even when you're not in that environment; if you're late one morning or take the day off, you may find yourself stressed at the same hour you are usually sweating in traffic. Your body, therefore, becomes stronger than your mind.

When you seek to make genuine changes in your life, therefore, you must let go of your past and train your emotions to be stronger than your environment. Breaking this cycle requires you to be conscious of your habitual routines and past experiences that create unconscious emotional reactions. In the "Inspired Action" part of this section, you will practice replacing dominant, restrictive habits with more conscious, intentional responses.

For now, let's take a step back and look at two common reactions: fear and avoidance. As you become conscious of what drives your life, you may notice how much your habits create who you think you are, and how much your habits limit you from being who you really are. Many people spend more time worrying about the unknown than doing what they love. By driving yourself toward the emotions you want to experience in the future, you align with the best version of your life.

CHAPTER 4
Your Higher Self

To know true freedom is to intimately know our chains.

—Anonymous

YOUR THOUGHTS ARE A CONTINUAL commentary on your daily life. When you look more closely at these thoughts, you'll notice that some reaffirm what you like and dislike and some completely contradict each other. It's all over the place, like a party with no guest list—everyone is invited, and it's free speech for all.

But your thoughts are not who you are. They do not define you, but rather project your experiences. If you often tell yourself that you are not good enough, it is usually because conditioning from your past triggers an emotion of inadequacy. But that's not reality—it just makes you *believe* you are not good enough. Your thoughts have power because they can make you act or feel a certain way. But they do not limit you because you can change them.

Your inner dialogue is like an endless stream of social media updates:

- I feel great today! #musthavebeenthecoffee

- I wish I had worn the black jeans today. #whatwasithinking

- Just got overtaken on the highway by a lady older than my grandma. #needforspeed

If you posted every "thought update" online, you would seem certifiably crazy. This consistent, unhelpful, often judgmental commentary shows that your mind decides what you like and dislike, what you agree and disagree with, so it can reinforce the construction of your ego.

Your ego holds beliefs about you, who you are, what you are good at. It loves to create emotional drama and longs to be reinforced constantly. Your thoughts accompany your ego on its mission to be "right," creating comfort zones so you don't stray from "who you are." But those thoughts are fabricated. They are based on your conditionings and experiences, and perhaps reinforced by influential elements from your parents and other important people in your life.

Whether you say you are introverted or extroverted, bold or cautious, pessimistic or optimistic, your life manifests the result of these beliefs. You see everything in your life as a reflection of yourself because your conditioning gives life its meaning. Where one person sees a possibility for failure, another might see an opportunity for growth. One person might learn from a failure, but for another, it will confirm their belief that *they* are a failure. Everything in your life reflects your individually programmed personality and unique past.

ဆာ)ၹ

So if you are not your thoughts—who are you?

First, you have to work with what you have been given. You must make peace with the challenges and privileges with which you have been gifted. Both can be used as stepping-stones to change rather than as excuses to validate your failures. Your ability to detach from them will allow you to see who you really are.

Second, you have to acknowledge an element that has been part of every moment of your life: your eternal, limitless, ever-present consciousness. This is the part of you that is always in a state of awareness, the silent space that cuts vertically through the endless mind-chat. You are conscious, and like a divine mother watching over her sacred child's life, you observe your life as it is lived before you. Your consciousness is the thin veil between the physical world and the non-physical; it is your connection to the source and energy that created you.

Some people translate this energy as the best version of themselves, their higher selves, and ultimately, their connection to the universe. Consciousness is your tool to connect with your higher self and these two elements are what make up the real you, the essence of who you are. Your connection with consciousness is found through daily, mindful awareness, meditation, and creativity.

When you concentrate on activities that require attention, you tap into consciousness. This state of mind gives you a dependable wholeness that both grounds you and gives wings to your freedom. When you connect to conscious awareness, you recognize that your higher self and your true self are the same. When you use consciousness instead of analysis to make decisions, you come from a place of true intent that allows you to navigate life with ease, focus, and empowerment. The more you detach from the illusion that your thoughts define you, the more you can embrace your limitless possibilities, and the freer you become.

Recognize that your thoughts are a commentary on your life, and that they have been manipulated by your environment, conditioning, and associations. They do not define you, but they do play a very important role in how you perceive your world. They support your ego with habits that create your life cycle. If you want more freedom to do what you love and to spend more quality time with those you love, you must change your restricting thoughts and emotional patterns. This is done by raising your vibration through conscious choice of how you want to live in and leave the world, which will be presented in Part Two. Take inspired action and practice your connection to conscious awareness by making decisions and changes based on intent, rather than on habit or predictability. This is how you will break the old patterns that have kept you stuck.

The next chapter will be your guide to creating inner freedom. It is the foundation on which you will start to build an abundant, high-vibrational, and intentional life. This guide does not require or expect perfection but encourages you to embrace your imperfections. To flourish, you must first get down into the dirt, so welcome these challenges with an open and curious mind.

Remember, you are here to discover, let go, and sift out what does not serve you, so you are left only with potent, conscious living.

CHAPTER 5
Your Inspired Actions

Travel doesn't become adventure until you leave yourself behind.

—*Marty Rubin*

INSPIRED ACTIONS OPEN THE DOOR to your consciousness, enabling intentional thoughts, emotions, and actions. These require awareness, focus, and freedom—the potent foundations of an inspired life.

Inspired actions also reflect efforts toward abundant receiving. This means embracing the unknown and surrendering to the energies in life that you cannot control. By adjusting to the organic flow of life and your changing environment, you are able to find stability within your higher self, rather than be swept away by the flux of external forces.

As you read this chapter, focus on each inspired action individually. They are sectioned into days, but you can combine them according to how much time you have—you can do two or three in one day if time allows, or perhaps fill up a two-week calendar with all the steps you find here; additional materials are available on my website, www.sezkristiansen.com. All are highly effective spiritual and psychological practices on the path to self-empowerment. By engaging in all twelve regularly, you will gain insight into your life and your inner workings that will lead to personal liberation.

Repeat these for as long as they nurture you into a state of awareness. Soon they will become an indispensable part of your personal growth and a platform from which you will be able to intentionally manifest an incredible life from.

Journaling: Free the Pen

For as long as I've been able to write, I have kept journals. They followed me all over the world and became a portal to places I had forgotten or longed to revisit. When I became a mother, I sat down and read through my journals with new eyes. Within the pages, I found my true free-spirited nature, but also noticed that I was often wrapped up in my own little world with a general lack of awareness.

In the first week after my son's birth, I decided to keep another type of journal. I bought a beautiful book hand-embroidered with the words "free spirit," and a fine black pen. I started by writing a few lines about my inner life every day: challenges, analysis of who I was as a person, my thoughts, childhood memories, meditation experiences, lucid dreams, and moments of pure gratitude. In only a few weeks I noticed the emotional difference that writing this way made.

Over the last few years, my journal has been my personal search engine and intravenous system through which I get nourishment and clarity every day. It became so fundamental in creating my intentional future that I literally burned all of my old ones. As I did so, standing over the flames of my old dreams and the old me, I felt free. It was as if I had rewritten myself into another life, one in which I was compassionate, empowered, and fully awake.

❧ ☙

The first step in freeing your mind is to disconnect from the sources that feed your habitual thought patterns and the conditioning or experiences that cause you to believe certain things. The best way to do this is to simply become more aware of the thoughts that cause you discomfort, pain, or fear. This lets you dig down to your roots and rebuild on more conscious and nurturing ground.

You may feel that you don't have ten minutes each day to check in with yourself on paper, but I encourage you to extract that time from an activity that does *not* serve who you want to be any longer. Perhaps it's the coffee date with the friend who saps your positivity, or the habitual TV series that you watch every night. Having a tangible record of your personal journey will be your single-most important gauge of progress.

You might be amazed to find how many themes in your life stem from the same cycle of thoughts and emotions, the same merry-go-round of actions and reactions. Without the introspection offered by journaling, it is impossible to see these themes clearly. Journals illuminate unconscious habits and give you the opportunity to see your mind-matter in third person, which creates conscious awareness and gives you back more control over your thoughts.

Your journal doesn't need to be a grand biography; it should be more an objective set of notes about someone for whom you care deeply and wish the highest inner well-being: yourself. This combination of compassion and objectivity will help you step back from your emotions, consciously select the thoughts and beliefs that serve you, and let go of those that don't.

When you choose your journal, make it inspiring—something you will actually want to write in—and find a pen that is easy to use. Keep your journal with you so you can jot down your observations at any moment; it may become an efficient way of dealing with stress caused by overthinking. These simple choices will make it much easier to return to your inner work every day.

Begin by noticing your thought patterns, which are a key driver of habit.

Day 1: Journal your thoughts for a day.

Pay attention to your thoughts today. Record them as a third person, neutral observer, unattached to the drama. You are observing your thoughts, not judging them, so don't feel ashamed or guilty if you find that some are disturbing. These are vital clues to uncovering your deepest beliefs; try to see them as breadcrumbs that could lead you to your ultimate liberation. Openness to this inspired action is key. It brings the light of awareness to an inner world where you have lived your whole life, but in which you have rarely been present.

When you have journaled your thoughts for the day, see if you can discern any patterns. Remember: Don't be hard on yourself for what you are thinking.

- How do you perceive your life right now?

- Do you see something for which you should take responsibility?

- Are there situations in which you see yourself as a victim?

Seeing yourself as a victim is a very common theme. It stems from a perception that something is happening *to you*, rather than understanding it as something that *you made happen.*

You have chosen everything in your life, consciously or unconsciously. Deciding to take full responsibility for how you live from now on—every single aspect of it—is one of the biggest steps you can take toward inner freedom. It is your initiation into conscious and intentional living, and one that will change your life irrevocably. The more conscious choices you start to make, the more you will be able to create positive, lasting transformations in your life.

When I first did this inspired action, I was on my maternity leave and my "thought-awareness days" were often filled with a mix of sleep deprivation, depression, and guilt for not doing enough. In hindsight, I would have loved to let go of those emotions and allow myself to laugh at my exhaustion a little more. One of my early entries went like this:

I often play the victim in my situations by saying things like, "I have no friends here, I have no family here." I am so tired all the time. I wish I had more energy to go to a yoga class or try something different. I haven't tried my best to fit in here. I must be more present with my child. I also spend a lot of time making statements about myself, like:

- *"I need to live by the water, it's where I belong."*

- *"I am not an outgoing person. I hate social situations; I wish I lived on an isolated island."*

I have conversations in my head with people I have to email, text, call—like I am rehearsing before I am able to take action. I notice I never look up or around when I walk in the city. Someone started talking to my son and I wasn't open enough to even smile or talk back.

I'm not very nice to myself! I tell myself what I should be doing, what I shouldn't be doing, what I don't deserve, why I don't have what I want, why I never will. If I have a confrontation with someone, my mind will replay it over and over again, telling me what I should have said, should have done instead. I question my husband and what he is doing with the baby, often commenting in my head about what I would do. My son was screaming while I was trying to make dinner and I had a moment where I just wanted to slam my hands down on the table and shout "I need peace!" but then my mind quickly reminded me of the guilt and remorse I would have for letting that one slip out. Sometimes I am reminded of my childhood by a smell or an image and I get caught in a confusing state of longing, a feeling of being lost, and the feeling that I am living someone else's life, not one I created myself.

Your journal entries can also take the form of poems. Poetry is a creative way of making sense of the world and has been used for centuries as a tool for healing the soul. It's a great way to condense your thoughts and emotions into just a few sentences. You don't need to be a profound poet, nor do you need to place any emphasis on format, style, or grammar—just be mindful of how you feel and bring that into your words.

Here are some tips on writing poetry that you can use in conjunction with your objective journaling.

- Start by taking a few deep breaths. Calm your mind by focusing on the air going in and out of your nostrils. Become aware of how you feel in yourself, whether you are content or if something is weighing on your mind. You can choose to write about how you feel right now or write about something that is affecting your ability to live fully.

- Try to deeply engage with your emotions, allowing yourself to become present without judgment.

- Write down whatever comes to mind. Describe a strong emotion using as many descriptive words as you can. Metaphors are a good way to portray how you feel. For example, you could say, "I feel a deepness, as if I were made of indigo oceans." It doesn't need to make sense or be logical, and it doesn't need to follow a rhythm. It just needs to come from you and your way of thinking.

- Really paint a picture of how you feel, breaking sentences where you would take a breath or where you would like to emphasize a word. Read it out aloud to yourself to see where themes can be made into stanzas (paragraphs or sections separated by a gap).

To expand poetry's potential to free your mind, try turning your poems into intentions. This means changing from a witness voice (words that acknowledge your emotions) to an intentional one (words that offer solutions). A witness poem might read like this:

I feel there is
so much resistance
in my day
and it conflicts
with all that
I wish to be.

Turn this into a solution-based, intentional poem by using your intuition or heart-center. For example:

Listen, learn, or let go.

That is what I choose
to ask myself
every time
I am met with
the resistance of life.

Listen, learn, or let go.

Detachment: Free the Chains

As you start becoming aware of your thoughts, you can begin to disengage from difficult emotions. Detachment is the ability to let go, even when your mind tells you to confront every aspect of that thought or emotion. This means every time you notice thoughts that judge, criticize, or blame, you need to step back and examine those thoughts. Detach and lean back into your place of consciousness, the place where you feel a connection to stillness, calm, and clarity. Imagine being seated in the back of your mind—your place of consciousness—and let that peace come to you. Stepping away from your thoughts and becoming aware of their empty content immediately loosens their grip, their power, and their authority. Sometimes you can even laugh at the internal drama and simply watch the madhouse, rather than being subjected to it.

Take a loving approach; don't demand your thoughts away or force them to stop. Instead, inspire them to dissolve in the light of consciousness. Your thoughts will never respond to force—that will only create more conflict. When you step back from them, do it gently. Let go of the struggle. You never want to feel that you are blocking yourself from your emotions. You can let them in and feel what they want to show you, but then allow yourself a moment of attention to assess their validity. Your aim is not to experience equanimity and happiness in every situation; it is your life's work to express yourself in the most beneficial way. This means stepping back from patterns that do not serve your higher self.

Day 2: Practice stepping back.

Use this day to lean back into consciousness whenever you feel caught up in an emotion, a conflict, or an uncomfortable situation. Set an hourly alarm to practice making your thoughts objective and watch them from a distance. If you feel emotional about something that happens, step back, take a moment to breathe, and come back into the situation with a response rather than a reaction. Allow time to connect to that place within that is neither calm nor defensive, but nothingness. Wait until you have reached this place before you return. This is the platform from which you can better see the situation and connect to your inner knowing of what to do. Every time you step back, notice how you feel. How does the situation resolve itself?

Don't view detachment as losing a part of who you are. Try instead to see it as distancing yourself from who you are not. Then step back into the eye of the storm, rather than be swept away by it. Consistent detachment will inspire so much energy back into your life that you may feel as if an emotional weight has been lifted and space within has expanded, allowing intention to flow without resistance.

When you move toward this liquid life, this flow that comes from being inwardly unanchored, gentle, and spacious, you move with the rippling fabric of existence. You will be able to connect to your higher self more easily and more often. The more you let go, the more you will rise. When you feel resistance, an impending confrontation, or stress, practice stepping back for a moment. Note your experience with your day of detachment in your journal. Did it help manage your emotions? Did it help you to respond rather than react?

Meditation: Free the Anchor

When I first began meditation, I had incredible experiences. They were filled with seemingly massive breakthroughs, flashing lights from the fabric of the universe, waves of ethereal energy filling my mind, body, and soul. It was only when I realized that I was unconsciously fantasizing my experience that I started to learn how to meditate more holistically.

For someone like me who has an overly imaginative mind, "real" meditation was disappointing at first. Only by grounding and connecting to myself in a quiet and gentle manner did it become truly beneficial. Learning to listen to my breath, to feel it in my body, to see the deeper, quieter connection I could form within myself was something that took quite a while. I kept wanting it to be something different, something that would hit me with "aha!" moments or reveal my hidden purpose. But that was not my experience. It took much more effort for me to be truly silent, to not judge the experience, to feel fully awake with eyes closed. When I had just a second or two of that indescribable feeling of nothingness, I finally came home to the familiarity of freedom.

You have probably heard about the benefits that daily meditation can provide. It reduces stress, helps to fight addictions, improves ability to focus, and promotes emotional well-being. But what you might not know is that daily meditation allows you to train your body to obey your conscious mind. Every time you make your body stay in one position without giving in to its habitual need to feed off external stimulation and distractions, you strengthen your consciousness.

This can affect your life in a number of ways. You can tap into conscious control more often, detach from your dominant habits, and start to believe that you are more content without the constant bombardment of taste, touch, sight, smell, and sound. This creates a grounding and deep connection within yourself.

So why is it so challenging to fit ten minutes of meditation into a day? While it's gratifying to see or feel positive results quickly, meditation doesn't work like that. Each sitting can bring a different experience, making it feel inconclusive, but that is where the actual benefit lies. Each time you sit to be still, to become gently aware of your breath, your state of mind, you bring something different to the mat. You wake up each day with different imprints from the day before and different perspectives as a result of the quality of sleep you just had (or didn't have).

Your emotional state depends on the ages of your children; their physical and emotional needs; your monthly cycle and hormone levels; and even substances such as caffeine, alcohol, and sugar. Your thoughts and emotions are transient, but even if you see your daily life as routine and predictable, it in fact contains subtle nuances of difference, depending on your emotional state.

This is why meditation is truly insightful, because through practicing it, you shed light on those subtleties and find revelations within them. Every time you sit, you face the challenge of letting go of your thoughts. Learning how to disarm them is a process, and that is why meditation is such an incredible training ground for detachment. When you detach, you rise. With time, you'll find it easier to practice the simple act of letting go, rising, and letting go again. It is how you untether yourself from your human experience and reach beyond the veil to your source and your higher self.

Meditation encourages you to accept yourself as you are: an ever-changing dynamic being. When you acknowledge your liquidity, you see that all life is flow and movement. The more you resist and conflict with that flow, the more you suffer. Resistance, which keeps you stuck in life, is released in meditation, allowing you to flow effortlessly.

There is no single practice that will make you a better meditator. Your ability to be open and present to each experience determines the degree of transformation you will experience. Whatever happens, try not to label the experience as good or bad; simply accept it. This will ensure that you continue the practice and form a habit that will become a decisive, invaluable tool in your intentional life.

When I was working overtime and dealing with an unbalanced period between my work and family life, I learned to cut ten minutes from my lunch break to gather some peace. I sat on a bench in a quiet corner and meditated for ten minutes. Doing this meant I didn't have to sacrifice time with my family or try to stay awake through an evening meditation.

We all have ten minutes pocketed somewhere in our day. See where you can gather these minutes and remember that meditation is an *energy-giving* activity, not an *energy-depleting* activity.

Day 3: Find 10 minutes to do a simple, grounding meditation.

Here is an exercise to get you started:

• Sit on the ground, using cushions to make yourself comfortable. Set a timer for ten minutes.

• Don't worry how it looks. Just find a position that makes you feel present and restful.

• Once you are comfortable, rub your hands together as quickly as you can to create some heat.

• Cover your eyes with your warm hands and take a few slow, deep breaths. Feel the warmth of your hands, feel the skin of your palms touching the curves of your face, and let your breath come to a natural rhythm without controlling it.

• After a few breaths, release your hands to a comfortable place on your lap.

• Inhale deeply three times, hold each breath for five heartbeats, and release.

• Now let your breath continue at its own pace. Notice if it is deep or shallow, quick or long. Feel the breath, the coolness as it enters your body—the light or heavy exhaust as it leaves your nostrils.

• If a thought comes up, gently acknowledge its presence and let it drift away again, releasing it like a balloon rather than driving it away by force. If you get caught by the thought for a few moments, practice coming gently back to the sensations of the breath.

• Once you find that you can release the thoughts, noises, or feelings that catch your attention, just sit with the feeling of being. Feel your body, its mass, its heaviness; discover which points of your feet connect with the ground. Notice how it is in constant movement— your breath, the blood in your veins, your beating heart. You are solid but dynamic. Sit with this feeling of solidity and strength as well as flow and openness.

- To complete the meditation, place both hands over your heart, one on top of the other. Feel your heart beating within your body, the light pumping motion beneath your skin and bones. Acknowlege the subtle and vibrant life flowing within.

- Thank yourself sincerely for taking the time to do this practice. Thank the universe, God, or source of energy for this beating heart that gives you life. Know that your heart is free from your rational mind. It has its own deep, knowing, and nourishing energy.

- Take three deep inhales, holding them for five seconds each before releasing.

- When you hear the timer go off, finish the meditation with an affirmation, or bow your head to conclude your experience.

If any significant thoughts arose during the meditation, write them down. This can make letting go of negative thoughts much easier because you can shed the light of conscious awareness on them. If you experience an emotion but don't know why it came to you, write it down and dig deep for any possible reasons you feel this way. Was it pulled out from your subconscious by something currently happening in your life? Or does it come from a past experience that has not found closure?

Sometimes it's easier to enter a particularly disturbing thought or emotion in your journal and draw a circle around it. From there, you can segment the rest of the page into "slices" leading from the circle. Inside each segment write possible origins for this disturbing thought or emotion. For example, if the emotion was "fear," then dig down into all the fears you currently have and write them in the slices. Maybe you have a fear of the unknown, and you're being pushed out of your comfort zone. To resolve this emotion, see whether you need to take action by acknowledging your fear or simply letting go of it.

Meditation can give you a deeper, more trusting connection to your true nature and provide an environment in which you can practice letting go. As hard as it can be sometimes, when you consciously acknowledge your thoughts during meditation and then let them go, you allow yourself to manifest a life based on potency and priorities. This acts as a filter, allowing only things that serve, nourish, and guide you to come through. Your emotions become a servant to your mind, and not the other way around. With this power, you are able to create conscious, life-transforming habits.

Letting go is an act of self-empowerment that will change your life. It lets you control both the things you focus on and the things you choose to let go. With only a few minutes of meditation a day, you will be able to use this practice in your daily life. The sudden rush of thoughts that usually sweep you off your feet and carry you into emotional drama will become less and less frequent. Before long, those destructive, critical thoughts will become a faint whisper, and you will be free to choose the thoughts that manifest the best version of your life.

As meditation creates a place in which positive, self-empowering thought and soul guidance can flourish, you may also notice that your ability to detach and prioritize becomes more prevalent. This greatly affects the way you see yourself and the way you navigate your life. The point is not to eliminate all challenges and create a consistently euphoric existence, but to work with what you have and who you are. When you focus on the light within, you release everything that does not resonate with your best self and shed the light of awareness on all that you are.

Reactive thoughts and autopilot reactions are your inner chains. Meditation reveals them in their true form; passive, transient, and subjective. It allows you to detach from everything that's kept you from consciously creating your best version of reality.

Reconditioning: Free the Habit

If you want to see how habits rule your life, try changing the location of your kitchen rubbish bin. You may find yourself dumping leftovers on the floor or whirling around in confusion before you remember that it's now next to the fridge instead of by the sink. To really up the game, try relocating all of your unconsciously used items: your alarm clock, the coffee, your shoes. If you are like most people, you will find it difficult to remember where they are.

Everyone is made up of unique imprints. While you may be largely unaware of their sources, they have nevertheless shaped your life and beliefs. I, for example, am deeply conditioned to seek vast outdoor spaces and warm climates because that is an environment in which I felt free in the past. Now I live in Scandinavia, a place that stands in enormous contrast to that conditioned preference. Despite my firm belief that I could never be happy in a cold climate, I fell in love with a Dane and had to choose between my conditioning and my soul mate. I have spent years "re-imprinting" myself, not just to survive the winters but to forge a deeper connection within myself that is unconditional, and I am pleased to report that even the most stubborn beliefs are capable of change.

When you want to become the best version of yourself, take a look at the habitual thoughts that fuel your daily outcomes. Here's a common example: "I am not good/clever/pretty/wealthy enough." If you make this type of negative statement about yourself, step back and remember that it is just your mind projecting its own opinion; it's not true. Remind yourself of the traits that make you proud of who you are and try to identify what made you think this judgmental thought. Was it seeing someone you envy? Did you experience some kind of rejection in the past that is being reflected in this moment?

In the following exercise, get to know your triggers and learn how to shift your reaction from powerlessness to conscious strength.

Day 4: *Shift your reactive patterns.*

The easiest way to get rid of one habit is to exchange it for another. You don't need to force out or banish your negative thoughts. You just need to gently detach yourself from them, and then become aware of something else. Like breaking up a toddler tantrum, distraction is key.

Your reactive patterns probably occur like this:

- Trigger: Something causes you to relive an experience from the past

- Reaction: Subconscious emotional response is repeated until it becomes a habit

- Outcome: Some form of resistance, avoidance, or fear gives power to that trigger

- To change the outcome, change the input:

- Trigger: Something causes you to relive an experience from the past

- Response: Step back for a moment, acknowledge the trigger, identify why it makes you emotional

- Outcome: Detachment and the ability to shift your attention elsewhere to disempower the trigger

Spend a day identifying your triggers. You will know you have been triggered when you have a strong negative emotional reaction to something you see, smell, touch, hear, or taste. You might be reminded of a past experience, or you might not know why you feel the way you do. If you find yourself in a state of stress, sadness, or anxiety, go through the process above and change your reaction.

You do not have to coexist with the demons of your past. You simply have to disempower them by being aware of their presence, and then let them go with love. When you do this consistently, your mind will literally rewire itself to replace negative reactions with positive, intentional responses.

Habits are the power behind our manifested lives. Changing them requires doing unexpected things outside your normal behavior. Conscious time is much more efficient than habitual time, so understand that if you continue to be conscious of your habits, you will have the energy you need to create a life of freedom.

Try not to let your journey become solely focused on the destination. Allow these bumps, stones, cracks, and dips to enable your inner strength and resilience. Remember: No easy road ever leads to a magnificent destination.

Mindfulness:
Free the Past and the Future

My son started daycare as soon as I took up work again. I felt our connection slip away, so I decided to make "Mama and Mathias time" once a week. Sometimes it was just a morning, while other times it was a whole day; I devoted time to just being with him and doing whatever he wanted.

Have you ever followed a toddler down a road with no agenda, no time frame, and nowhere to go? It takes you to places and moments you could never imagine. It also takes a lot of patience.

At first, I simply could not understand why we had to stand and look at a crack in the concrete for twenty minutes, but once I let go of my conditioned need to "be somewhere" and surrendered to curiosity, it was magical. I could really see, with the eyes of a child, the appeal of this crack in the ground. Once I got down to his level, I saw a stream of ants filtering in and out, and the determined growth of a dandelion. Perhaps my son was thinking, "Where are they going? Does an ancient ant city lie below? Is the dandelion their marker so they know where to find their home again?" If you play with these possibilities for even a moment, your perspective changes, and you can see that it is much more than "just" a crack in the road. This is a great example of mindfulness and how it can change your view of the world. As you rush through your days to get to places you need to be, you miss the magic in the minutiae. This is what mindfulness is in its essence: slowing down, drawing all your senses into the moment, and feeling truly alive.

"Mindfulness" has been simplified into a misleading buzzword that means to be focused or aware. But it is much more than that. To be mindful means to be fully aware of all the elements in the present moment, observing the smells, touch, sounds, sights—everything that is happening—without labels, without expectations.

You want to be mindful of your thoughts, because you know that they tend to run off on their own trajectory. You want to be mindful of your actions because they can cause a great deal of harm to both yourself and others. You want to be mindful of your speech and how you use your energy. Being consistently mindful sheds light on moments you might otherwise miss because of your consistent need to be somewhere, do something, or achieve something.

For mothers, mindfulness is an incredible tool (especially if meditation isn't an easy option): It shows you how you can balance your personal life with motherhood. Balance is not a scale weighing one element against another; it is an inner pendulum that falls into equilibrium with deep connection to the present moment. So, when you are at work, *be* at work. When you are with your children, *be* with them. When you are in a moment of self-care, *be* fully present for the experience of self-nourishment.

When I first started practicing mindfulness in a Buddhist school, I did not know the impact it would have on my life, let alone on my relationship with my children. I practiced being present a few times a day, first by associating it with the action of making a cup of tea. I was triggered into mindfulness whenever I made a cup of tea by putting a sticky note that said "mindful" on my teacup. The message reminded me that I was to make the tea with as much sense-awareness as possible. I smelled the loose tea leaves, imagining the hands that picked them and the sunlight and rain that crafted the perfect environment. I poured the hot water as carefully as I could, watching the swirls of steam and imagining what it would be like not to have such easy access to this life-giving water. After a couple weeks, I started relying less on the reminder and began to be more "awake" in all my moments.

Life takes on an incredible awakeness when you live with mindful awareness. It's as if the world comes alive and all the elements that make up a moment are vibrating in front of you. You suddenly notice the small things—like a paper bag dancing in the wind or the sunlight as it catches a window. These small and yet extraordinary moments start to make you realize the beauty in simplicity, and you become truly grateful for them.

You can even be mindful in a stressful situation with your children or your spouse. Mindfulness can make the moment less reactive and more responsive. You think a little more about how you want to reply rather than allowing a reactive habit to take over.

Just as you can exchange one habit for another, you can make mindful awareness your default state by practicing a few times each day: as you wipe the table after dinner, make a warm drink in the evening, or sit in silence after the house is quiet. Each of these can do an enormous amount of soul-nourishing when practiced as conscious rituals rather than default habits.

The trick with mindfulness is not to judge any moment as good or bad, but to see the moment as it is. You can do this by stepping back into your place of consciousness and using your senses to experience the moment. Try this practice a few times each day and see how your energy changes throughout the week.

Day 5: Create a "mindful moment trigger" that you can use every day.

Think of a process or activity that you usually hurry through—making your morning coffee, preparing a cup of tea, or simply drinking a glass of water. Make this activity a mindful moment and spend five minutes more on it than you usually would. It's like "slow brewing" the moment to bring out its flavor.

As you do your activity, feel everything the moment has to offer.

- What do you hear?

- What can you see?

- What are the more subtle details?

- How do you feel within yourself at this moment?

- How does your physical body feel?

Take a breath, lower your shoulders, loosen your jaw, and feel your heart beating inside your chest while you do your activity. Think of all the people that have contributed to making the products you are using: the people working in the factories, their daily lives, their children. Think about the environment it took to create the material or product you are about to use: the sun, the warmth, the rain, the technology. Try to imagine all these elements and think about how intricately intertwined we all are. This moment is not just yours; it was cocreated by many lives.

It takes practice and constant little nudges to break your habitual chain of thoughts and busyness, but when you do, it's like surfacing into a world that is truly free from your own influence.

When I began this practice, I began to realize how infrequently mindful I was. This further woke me to how I was actually living and how I had spent my years of traveling. I then installed an app on my phone to help me be more mindful. When the bell rang, I wrote down how I was feeling, what I was thinking, and how "present" I was in that moment.

Many studies indicate that when you concentrate on only one activity, you are significantly happier than when you try to do many things at once. Therein lies the truth of mindfulness: When you are truly mindful, you cannot feel the sadness from your past or experience anxieties for the future, because neither exists in that perfectly present moment.

This is the key to womanhood: Be mindful to what the moment requires. If it requires that you wear the hat of an employee, partner, friend, daughter, spiritual being, mother— simply be mindful with that task and don't mix it with another. You probably know the perils of trying to get a little work done while looking after small children. It's a recipe for stress, temper tantrums, and inefficiency.

In mindfulness, you slow down. You acknowledge that your life exists within the chaos and the moments you are rushing through. Slowing down creates more space for freedom because you cannot be mindful quickly. You may feel you are too busy to slow down, but the more mindfully you spend your life, the more efficient you will be. Intentional living is found in the practice of mindfulness.

Next time you are with your child, look deeply into their eyes and listen to what they say, look at what they want to show you, respond deeply and with compassion for their innocence, whatever their age. What a difference this can make to your connection with them! When you are truly present with your child, you slow time. Your presence in life's little, everyday moments is freedom from unnecessary, conditioned hurriedness. You gain the ability to create more time with your family and be more efficient with your work. Slow down, look up and around, find the beauty in little things, and become present in a world of infinite curiosities.

Compassion and Gratitude: Free the Judgment

There's nothing like motherhood to light the flame of compassion. You feel it as soon as you know you're pregnant—it's a red thread that connects you to all women. It's your initiation into becoming a mother and caring for your child. As compassion takes over, you feel deeply empathic toward those who suffer and immensely grateful for your own life.

When your thoughts turn away from your own problems and toward those of others—be they family, friends, or strangers—a remarkable alignment with your higher self can occur. You begin to act in accordance with your true, potent nature and not your dilutive conditionings. Compassion reflects oneness and interconnection with all living beings. In compassion, you love without expectation and give without needing anything in return.

It's important to be conscious of your compassionate nature, however. Although it has the potential to connect and inspire you, it can also drain you by allowing you to absorb sensitivities that are not yours to take on.

ॐ

Before I started my transformation through intentional living, I spent twelve years in marketing. I worked for a variety of companies all around the world, creating content for clients such as the British Army and Scandinavia's largest lingerie company, as well as multinational surf and lifestyle companies. At brainstorming meetings, my clients and I would create proposals designed to get customers to consume the most goods in the least time.

I learned intimate, predictive details about our customers. I learned who they were. I learned how they felt—that they were never satisfied, that insecurity could be thwarted by the purchase of a certain product, that it would make everything OK, make them fit in, make them feel good about themselves, make them belong, if only they had this item, this perception of freedom.

My career made me realize that I had to examine the beliefs I was going to teach my children. Did I want them to be the "ideal customer?" Did I want them to believe they were not enough? Did I even want them to be predictable, conformed, or "normal" if it meant they lost a piece of their uniqueness?

Advertising is not the source of all evil, but it is a major, influential element of Western culture. It has changed global perceptions of certain behaviors and aesthetics. Advertising thrives on insecurity, so being confident in yourself is a rebellious act!

If you spent more time becoming aware of the people who produce the items you buy and chose more ethical and environmentally-conscious sources, it would be a great step toward compassionate living. Being aware of how products have been made and the conditions in which they have been produced can connect you to everything you own. Wearing clothing made possible by child labor in conditions you would never tolerate for your own children is vibrationally different from wearing an item sourced from an ethical, sustainable, and fair environment.

When I look out into the world and see other women going through motherhood in different conditions, I am very grateful for all that I have. Even when I feel like I don't have much, there is always someone going through something unimaginably worse. For acutely sensitive people like me, the burden of compassion can sometimes be so overwhelming that it is difficult to read the news or confront the world's inequality.

But compassion and gratitude can be enabling tools that free others. By acknowledging the injustice of the world and taking it in without turning away or being broken by it, you can acquire the strength to help others. Practicing compassion also makes you more aware of the freedom that is already yours.

Day 6: Make compassion a daily practice.

Practicing compassion is like trying to light a fire in a storm. Your match has to be sheltered from the wind and rain. Once the kindling has been lit, the little flame has to be nurtured. Only when it becomes a magnificent bonfire can it withstand the elements on its own.

Your matches are little acts of kindness, performed with sincerity, that come from compassionate understanding. This is the path of true spiritual growth. School drop-off and pick-up times are always a good place to start, because that's where you meet other parents, each on their own inner journey. You can always tell who's had a bad day, who's deeply unaware and never looks up, who's busy on their mobile while scurrying their kids out. When you smile or say "hi" with sincerity, you suddenly break them from their autopilot routine, offering them a moment of your presence.

Some will return your gesture. Others won't even notice. But the more you do this, the more you will notice how this act becomes a little ray of light that shines through the shadows. Remember, people reflect their own inner worlds; their reactions are never a judgment on you. If others make you feel insecure for having the capacity to open yourself up, then take a moment to remember you are creating light in a world that already has too much darkness. Like the sun that does not choose the people it shines upon, you can be a moment of unexpected light in someone's day; you may never know how much it might affect or help them. Doing this takes practice and resilience. There are many people around you who need a little light, and very few are willing to give it without expecting that it will be returned.

Compassion starts with those around you. By becoming conscious of others' needs, and by performing small, selfless acts, you will be reminded of your oneness with the world. When you start to focus on others, your own problems take up less of your time. This puts energy back into your life, gives you a break from incessantly trying to fix yourself, and opens you to a new perspective.

೮೧೮೩

Most mornings, my daughter and I drop my son off at school, then walk a short distance back through the city. We stop at the same crossing light, where we meet the same old man standing outside in his pajamas every morning. As we live in a city that has more bikes than pedestrians, we stand on the sidewalk and watch the endless stream of cyclists rush by. My daughter has taken it upon herself to wave at everyone, shouting "*god morgen!*" while we wait for the light to change. My heart fills with a little sadness, because hardly anyone acknowledges her sweet, chubby little hand as it waves ferociously. But I also admire her ability to persist without needing a response.

As my daughter and I perform this ritual of smiling and waving every morning, I feel as if we are the stillness amid chaos at that stoplight. As the old man pulls a remote control out of his pajama pocket to "switch the red man to green," I cross the street filled with gratitude for the awareness of others that I have in my life.

Day 7: Practice gratitude through journaling.

Gratitude is easy when you can see good things in your life. But what about when life gets tough? It's likely that you spend more time thinking about what you lack than you do acknowledging what's good. This warps your perspective, because it frames your life as devoid of something, rather than as inherently whole. Gratitude means having a holistic perspective that sees things from all angles. As you learned earlier, changing perspective is key to consciously free living.

Gratitude is a practice, just like mindfulness. See the present moment as it is, and thank it for giving you everything you need: your heart, your lungs, the ability to think for yourself. Even in difficult times you can choose gratitude and see your challenges as experiences that will lead to spiritual growth and inner resilience.

Using your journal, take a step toward creating a platform based on appreciation and deep acknowledgement for all you have. Take a few moments each day to express your gratitude for the day's events and experiences. You could also spend time on a Sunday listing everything you were grateful for that week. Make it a practice with your family—have them tell you three things that made them happy. It is truly enlightening to hear their responses, discover their simple satisfactions, and gain a glimpse of life as they see it.

Physical: Free the Body

Using your body to free your mind is an incredible way to accelerate your personal growth. Whatever state your body is in right now—whether you've recently birthed children or been a mother for many years—it is a beautiful reminder of your selflessness in nourishing another life. When you move your body, every muscle of it, you create a measurable "feel-good" vibe that not only helps you live longer but releases stored negative energy.

Regular exercise also improves self-esteem. This is why it is such a good outlet when you are faced with difficult situations, because it rebuilds your confidence. When you exercise, your nervous system releases a group of hormones called endorphins. These act as analgesics, which reduce the perception of pain. I strongly believe endorphins relieve not only physical pain, but emotional and psychological pain as well. Their release feels like a natural high, so it makes sense that regular exercise could diminish difficult emotions linked to anxiety and depression.

ℰↄℭ

There were times in my life when I suffered with anxiety, panic attacks, and complete disconnection from myself, a state of mind that caused many detrimental physical effects. When I look back on photos of those times, I find myself completely unrecognizable, a shadow of who I was to become.

I didn't know then that physical health and mental health are connected at a fundamental level, and I had little relatable knowledge that could have inspired action. It was only when I gave my body to bearing children that I saw how respecting and intuitively caring for my body would nourish my mind in return.

Between full-time work and caring for my toddler, it became increasingly difficult to fit running into my everyday life—especially in the Nordic winter. So I decided to try something different: I bought a pass to a local yoga studio. Classes took place after "baby bedtime" hours, and the social aspect made it easier to commit when I knew other people were going through the same balancing act.

I soon realized that the mindset I brought to class depended on the day I'd had. Like meditation, exercise magnifies your mindset: You can either consciously apply it to your activity, or you can allow it to overpower you and create a negative experience. Exercise is an indicator of how you deal with life's difficult situations. Do you usually make excuses, or do you show up and give it all you have?

Exercise teaches you how to deal with the conflict between what your mind tells you and what you can actually accomplish. You will always have excuses for why you can't do things, but you must not let them bind you to a life that does not reflect your limitless potential. If you allow yourself to be limited by your excuses, you will forever be stuck in a pattern of habit that gives you the exact life you have right now.

If you want to change, if you want to be the conscious creator of your own life, then you must free yourself from the restriction of excuses. The beauty of this is that it takes only twenty-one days to exchange a poor habit for a good one. In less than a month you can integrate the tool of exercise in your life, and it will create exponentially more physical and emotional energy and well-being.

Yoga is one way to balance the body and the mind, and all you need is internet access to take a class. But any type of physical activity can channel emotions through movement, regardless of your body type or fitness level.

Day 8: *Free your mind through movement.*

The body you have right now is all you have to carry you through this lifetime, so move it in any way you can, as often as you can. Mothers have busy lives, but many daily activities can be turned into exercise. In addition, this inspired action is intended for the mind as well as the body, so try to incorporate any stresses, troubles, or challenges you currently have into your activity. Use your body to release tension by putting your mind into your body and working it out.

Here are a few ideas that might help raise your heart rate during the day:

- What exercise did you love as a child or teenager? See if you still enjoy it.

- Forget the car for a day and walk.

- Don't follow the crowd on escalators and elevators—take the stairs and enjoy the space.

- Put on your favorite song and dance.

- Explore a part of your neighborhood by foot, getting as lost as you can. Try to find your way back without navigation.

- Let your children ride their bikes to a park while you jog alongside them.

- Try a yoga class in person or online.

- Exercise with a friend who will help you commit to your routine.

As you exercise, don't just focus on the physicality of the movement; observe your mind as well. What insecurities, emotions, or habitual thoughts come up? Do you often give up when it gets too hard, telling yourself you can't do it? Or do you push through, assuring yourself that you are capable?

Every time you feel like giving up, encourage yourself to go a little longer or try a little harder. See what happens to your self-confidence once you push through even a couple of times. Make a note of your accomplishments, even the little ones, in your journal. Take a photo of yourself every time you do something your mind said you couldn't. This is how you recondition your mind to associate empowerment with exercise and how you become resilent in the face of other life challenges.

Reflect on your entries after twenty-one days and ask yourself if your mental response to exercise reflects how you deal with the rest of your life. If you find some difficult answers, keep using exercise to refine them. Keep telling yourself that you are capable and that you are not defined by your thoughts.

Nature: Free the Wild

Regular access to nature is linked not only to a significant decrease in depression and anxiety, but it also benefits physiological well-being. Many people have rediscovered ancient techniques such as forest bathing and grounding as forms of therapy. It can help those of us prone to the winter blues and may also be therapeutic for some types of stress disorders. Perhaps science is catching up with what our ancestors knew; nature holds many secrets for mental health and spirituality, and it may be more necessary than ever now that we spend many hours a day in front of screens.

Too often, self-worth is validated through external sources such as social media, but nature can be an antidote to this psychological disconnection. No app can make you truly understand the smallness and fragility of your life. Nature holds your roots, your ties to the past, and mysteries connected to the depths of your soul. Nature holds every speck of existence that has ever come into being, perished, and passed into the earth on which you stand. Nature holds everything you need to pursue inner freedom and spiritual fulfillment, and it's something many of us need more of as we grow older.

ℋℂ℁

I was very close to nature as a child, but when I became a student and moved to the city, I had neither the time nor the funds to travel. In the urban landscape, I never noticed the seasons, the ever-changing nuances of nature's cycles. When I began to feel this void, I filled it with low-vibe choices and feel-good quick fixes, as many students do.

I began to despise the rain and the cold and saw no worth in them. I heated up my tiny room and closed my windows and doors to the outside world. I created an artificial bubble that disconnected me from the thing I needed most. Avoiding nature became a habit. Soon I didn't know where my place was. I needed something to inspire me out of the cage I had constructed.

I believe that when you are most lost in life and need some true soul-nourishing, an opportunity will always come up to remind you of who you really are—you just need to be brave enough to take it. My opportunity came in the form of an advert from a local travel agency. It announced a sale on flights from London to Portugal for ninety-nine pence. I bought the ticket the same day.

For an entire summer, I lived in a cave in southern Portugal. It was like the pendulum of Tao swinging to the other environmental extreme to rebalance me. I spent my nights watching shooting stars and falling asleep to the sound of waves beating against distant rocks. I woke to the soft, salty dew that clung to my sleeping bag every morning. It was uncomfortable at times, but the freedom trumped any negatives. I shared that cave with some strange and wonderful people, brought together by the divine connection that lost souls usually have. I explored the surrounding region every day, often noting in my journal the flora and fauna I discovered. I lived very simply and potently, in harmony with my environment and myself.

When I returned to my education at the end of the summer, I realized how my life lacked this fundamental red thread of nature. Many years later, when I became pregnant for the first time, that thread became much more than just a concept. Nature was not external, but innate; it was the literal cord that provided life to an unborn child.

As mothers, we become nature herself. We create life and pass it to our children as a sacred gift. It doesn't take much to see the joy with which children react to rain puddles, snowy hills, and warm oceans. It takes less to see the curiosity that widens their eyes and melts their hearts when they are in contact with animals. That's where our curiosity comes from: our wish to discover what's under that rock, what lies over that hill, and what's beyond that body of water.

Here are some simple techniques you can use to rekindle your intimate relationship with nature.

Day 9: Spend time outside to ground yourself in nature.

Take a trip to the park or another green space and spend an hour grounding yourself. Sit mindfully with the soles of your bare feet on the grass. Look up into trees, at the patterned skies they create; notice the temperature, the colors, and the smells of the season. The wilder the nature, the freer you will feel, so try a more remote spot where you can feel the vastness of the environment.

Bring your children and experience nature with them, their way: Climb trees, lift rocks, take two hours to walk ten meters, and lie in the long grass, spotting magic dragons in the clouds. Stand with your back against a tall, wide tree and feel the energy it holds. Notice how strong and solid it stands, even as it bends slightly toward the top. Imagine yourself as this tree for a moment—grounded, rooted, and flowing with resilient inner strength. The tree bends a little with the pushes and pulls of life. When you encounter an unassuming wasp or spider, remember that nature is the host and you are the guest.

Here are a few tips on how to connect with nature in your everyday life:

- Use nature-based products like essential oils, organic skin care, and natural foods to create harmony between your mind, body, and the environment. When you can, use natural remedies for colds and flu.

- Track your monthly menstrual cycle with an app. Learn more about each stage so you can know when to be creative, when to be productive, when to reflect, and when to restore.

- Use the lunar cycle to affirm or manifest your goals. Cycles are a great way to connect to the nature that is all around you and within you, too.

- Buy plants instead of cut flowers and bring life into your living space. They not only replenish the air but also respond to the environment and nourishment you provide.

- Make your own kombucha. This ancient fermented drink has valuable health benefits and provides an incredible psychological link to your relationship with creation. There is nothing like a scoby[2] to connect you back to your motherly placenta.

Humans once lived by the ebbs and flows of the natural cycle, and you can reconnect with them by spending conscious time in nature. The freer and wilder your mind is (i.e., more conscious and creative), the more harmony you will find between your inner and outer worlds.

Humor: Free the Weight

The weight of responsibility can make motherhood feel quite heavy. You are liable not only for another human's physical growth, but also the well-being and development of their soul. You may feel this weight every day as you try to balance personal desire and commitment to your family, leaving very little space for spontaneity and humor.

Trying to explain the peculiarities of life to my children—things like the concept of religion, what existed before time, how babies are born—made me realize that the world is an incredibly delicate, intricate, and intelligent place. If you took just a moment to think about it all, you might just laugh a bit, too.

When you take a moment to step back, you realize that there are moments in motherhood that are worth laughing about—just try dealing with newborns or teenagers, for example. These experiences help you let go of the self-importance that limits personal growth. If you can learn to laugh at yourself, you'll spend a lot less time trying to preserve your ego and have a lot more emotional energy to spend on the things that matter.

---

[2]An acronym for "symbiotic culture of bacteria and yeast," used in the fermentation and production of kombucha, a fermented tea.

I was always very serious, even as a child. I wrote poetry about the injustice of the world. I wrote about poaching in South Africa. I wrote about old people and the loneliness they felt sitting in old-age homes. Writing allowed me to expel the hypersensitive thoughts and emotions that I carried with me like a bag of bricks. I had an unnatural level of worrisome thoughts, which tormented me in my dreams. I had precautionary routines for fearsome activities such as flying or being confined, and I spent a large portion of my life preparing for the worst. Only when I had my first child did I discover what was worth worrying about, and what was a waste of vital mental energy.

I knew I wanted to continue traveling with my children, and I discovered that about 20 percent of my worries regarding air travel with young children could be overcome by being pragmatic and prepared. The other 80 percent were emotionally draining and redundant thoughts that harmed my family and undermined the journey. The more I lightened up about what I couldn't control, the more of what I couldn't control turned out to be fun.

When you take life too seriously, when you worry about the little things, you chain yourself to an emotional anchor that burdens you with unnecessary restrictions, making it harder to flow, to be open, and to be truly present to all the wonder that lives in the now. Your burden remains heavy as long as you hold onto it—until you consciously begin to let go.

In the practice of letting go and lightening up, the art of humor is like adding helium to a lead balloon. Let's begin with a simple practice that provides some perspective.

Day 10: See the world from a child's angle and create your own perspective.

- When you are faced with frustration, stress, and pressure—from yourself, work or family—remind yourself of the shortness of life. Imagine seeing yourself, as you are right now, from a distance. Imagine ascending away from your situation, beyond the roof of your building, beyond the sky, beyond the atmosphere, and into the universe, where you are able to look down at your existence from a great distance.

- See just how big the world is—how it is populated with billions of other people, each one striving and competing to attain something. Imagine how many people have lived before you, and how many will live after. Think of the silliness of it all—the fact that you are even alive right now, on this little speck of dirt in a galaxy that is one of millions. See your life as but a second on a timeless clock. What really matters to you when you think of this? What does this situation really require from you—to let go and lighten up? To take inspired action toward change? Indulge in a little humor every day, and let a little space in.

- Try explaining some deep, universal concepts to your child and observe their reaction. Do they find them unimaginable, unbelievable, or purely outrageous?

- When you feel worried about something, ask yourself: "Can I change it?" If you can, then change it. If you can't, then practice detachment as we discussed on Day 2. If you want to change it but you feel you can't, then empower yourself with either action or knowledge, but don't wait in the middle. Every moment you spend in indecisiveness takes up a needless amount of mental bandwidth.

- If you find yourself in the depths of a dark ocean of seriousness, where life moves only in labored stillness, remember that freedom lies in recognizing your smallness in the world and understanding that you are a speck of existence in the universe. Choose to see the humor that weaves through all humanity, and remember that a little distance and a little humor is sometimes all you need to regain perspective.

- If you don't know how to find the humor and lightness in everyday life, spend time with a five-year-old. It's hard to sense impending doom in the presence of someone who wants to be a dog when they grow up. Humor helps you let go of the belief that you know everything, and children are marvelous educators who can show you that you actually know very little. You learn from them how to be alive, and how to see something again for the first time. To them, everything is worthy of attention, and of questioning.

Community: Free the Loneliness

The journey through motherhood and the drive to balance it with personal freedom can feel isolating.

In Buddhism, spiritual progress is not possible without a *sangha*, a community of like-minded people. The connections that make it possible to relate and share emotions with a supportive group is a sacred necessity on the path to enlightenment. Philosophers and scientists agree that sharing your journey helps extend longevity. Midwives recommend "mother groups" that allow women to share the joys and burdens of parenthood. These groups significantly reduce the chances of postpartum depression and other psychological disturbances related to childbirth.

As you progress in your spiritual and personal growth, it's natural to want to share the journey that has lifted you from the darkness and into the light. When you have a breakthrough during meditation, or if the simple power of mindfulness adds vibrancy to your day—you want to tell someone. The more transformational the experience, the deeper the desire to communicate it to others.

On the other hand, spiritual growth often brings with it some kind of loneliness. You may feel vulnerable sharing this personal journey with anyone—even a close friend—because you fear being judged. Or perhaps you feel that your insights are not understood. Don't be surprised by this. If your mind begins to question your path, it's important that you share your doubts and fears with loved ones. This allows new ideas to break up stale thoughts and adds a perspective that could be invaluable to your spiritual progress.

As you begin to free your mind through conscious awareness, you can also learn to embrace yourself without this restricting fear, and consciously choose your friends, a like-minded tribe that can share your journey.

ℰↃ☾ℜ

Even though I've lived in Denmark for several years now, finding a supportive group has been a big challenge. "Community" is a difficult subject for me, since I am quite introverted. I look for escape routes at social gatherings, and I prefer to hide among the houseplants rather than introduce myself at parties. As soon as I had children, however, I realized I would have to overcome my fears so they could attend birthdays and play dates. (This is another way that motherhood is liberating: By putting your children's needs first, you can overcome your anxieties and conditioned fears. This stops the chain of inherited psychological restrictions. What a marvelous gift to pass on to the next generation—the freedom to choose their own soul-nourishing habits!)

I was determined to find a tribe of women similar to myself, so I began my search: *Mother of two, open and experimental, culturally and socially mismatched, seeks spiritual conversations or adventures after the kids' bedtime.*

My many social efforts included creating a Meetup group for mindful mothers, attending multireligious choirs, meditating at different Buddhist centers, drinking cocoa at full-blood blue moon ceremonies, going on herbalist tours in botanical gardens, and attending vegan festivals and gong baths. I joined the local shaman's sweat tent, multilingual mothers' groups, various yoga studios, and the Philosophy Society. I went to pottery classes and became an evening intern at the immigrant art foundation.

From this search I learned that no one group of people fit my ideal of a like-minded "spiritual growth tribe" that could support me, encourage me, and make me feel less isolated. I discovered that community is not a specific group of similar people, but a collection of unique individuals with whom I could connect personally and share new ideas. It was immensely liberating and took the pressure off finding that one and only group that was supposed to be my "soul-tribe."

ℰↃ☾ℜ

As you start to replace your unconscious habits with new and nourishing patterns, you may notice that some people in your life don't nurture you. These people connect with you only through negativity, bitching, or judgment. When this becomes apparent, it's time to let go of their toxic energy. Through this you will rise emotionally, psychologically, and vibrationally.

If your personality is made up of the five people with whom you spend the most time, think about who contributes to who you want to be. Who doesn't? Ask yourself what you get out of those negative relationships and why you allow their energy to deplete you. Then consciously surround yourself with those who not only support and encourage you to be the best version of yourself, but also those who challenge your limiting beliefs with new perspectives.

Day 11: Find a community, a person, or a place that inspires your self-empowerment journey.

You must break down the walls of your restrictive comfort zone to meet new people—doing so will become the biggest asset in your intentional life. Since you mold yourself by the company you keep, join a group that inspires you to move in a new direction, or become a friend to someone who has bold, inspiring energy. My favorite approach to making new friends is to buy a good packet of freshly ground coffee and leave it for them with a note suggesting that you share it one morning.

Release your fear of rejection or humiliation—these are restrictions that keep your life from being lived at its highest potential. Go back to your detachment practice, and be open to learning something new about yourself. As you try this new way of relating, pretend that you are empowered and sociable. Remember that everyone is in the same situation, no matter how confident and capable they appear.

Places like yoga studios and meditation groups are great for meeting people who are interested in personal growth, but that doesn't mean they're on the same journey you are or that they're more open-minded than people in other communities. If you join a club, choose one that offers the most beneficial experiences rather than the most potential friendships. Focus on the activity and the friendships will follow.

Your path will not always take you to the people you want to meet—but you will meet more people who will help you learn what you need to know along the way. Take every person you meet as a teacher and treat strangers with curiosity. The less you are concerned about how they might respond to you, the more you will become aligned with your confident self and open to receiving empowering connections with others. You never know what a person or group might be able to teach you, or who they might become to you in the future. Try to never be diheartened by the assumption that someone doesn't want to connect with you. This can cause you the most suffering because you are needlessly hurting yourself with an idea rather than facts. Pursue in person friendships over online ones, and you will find it easier to see the other person's true intentions.

ℰℭ

I once went to a yoga festival in my early years of being a new, self-conscious mom. I was so excited to meet all these similar people, connect with interesting strangers, and perhaps even make a soul-friend or two. I tried my best to talk to everyone and even found myself in the vicinity of a well-known kundalini[3] teacher from Germany. She had just given a meditation and had mentioned her children, so I immediately felt that we shared a connection.

Once I was able to talk to her, I spent a few arduous minutes trying to start a conversation. But she was so dismissive and uninterested that I literally gave up and walked away feeling embarrassed and ashamed of myself. Later that week, I came across an article written by this teacher about spiritual loneliness. She said that because she was a spiritual teacher, people always assumed she was having a great day, always able to perform, and always up for a chat, when in reality she sometimes felt isolated and unable to shake off her inner turmoil.

This article made me realize that your perceptions of others—and of yourself—may be based on illusions. My imagined kinship with the yoga teacher is an example of this. If you can open your mind to potential friendships regardless of spiritual, cultural, or social preferences, you will see that freedom lies in the minds of those who are open enough to reach beyond their fears and judgments.

---

[3] A style of yoga that incorporates movement, breathing techniques, meditation, and chanting.

Mindset: Free the Foundations

Your mindset is your foundation; it is fundamental to the way you perceive the world, deal with difficulties, and ride the ebbs and flows of life. It is determined by what you believe in and what you believe is possible. If your mindset is guided by an unchanging set of values and perceptions, your life experiences will follow unsatisfying, repetitive patterns. Luckily, your mindset is not "set," but soft and malleable. Reframing it can help you shape an extraordinary life.

If you want to determine what your current mindset is, ask yourself, "How do I see life?" Does it hold meaning, purpose, and an abundance of possibility? Or does it constantly challenge you with conflict, lack, and impossibility? Whether you know it or not, you answer that question every day. Your choice is whether you do it consciously or unconsciously.

Choosing the way in which you wake up, with awareness of how you want the day to go, is one of the best ways to liberate your mind from habit and empower your life with intention. A morning routine that nourishes, grounds, and consciously connects you to your intentions sets the tone for the rest of the day.

I am a self-confessed ice maiden in the morning. The years I spent waking up innumerable times each night to feed, comfort, and occasionally revel in the somnolent beauty of my children have not brought me any closer to becoming a "morning person." After one of my typical nights of vivid, lucid dreams, I usually wake up feeling like an emotional trashcan. As a result, I began to wake up half an hour earlier and adopted the simple morning "reset" ritual below to free me from the night's lingering tentacles.

After a few weeks of waking up early, I realized I had overcome something else I thought I would never be able to change. I have literally created more time. For the first time in my life, I feel like I start the day, not that the day starts before me. Even better, my predawn hours are exceptionally productive; they gave me time to write this book—something I would never have been able to do before.

Day 12: Wake up 30 minutes earlier and develop an intentional routine.

The hour before the rest of the house wakes up is a sacred time. It can become a vital moment of peace, a quiet space for intention, and a chance to start your day with the right mindset. Set your alarm half an hour earlier than usual, and place it somewhere that requires you to get up to turn it off, so you won't be tempted to hit the snooze button.

Begin the day: Sit in a comfortable position. Ground yourself by placing your feet on the floor and taking a few deep breaths. Try to spend five minutes meditating—if you're sure you won't go back to sleep. If you're like me and find morning meditation a challenge, have a book nearby that you find uplifting and inspiring. Open to a random page and read the first few lines, reflecting deeply on the words.

Write your intentions for the day in your journal, writing what you would like to achieve in the middle of a page, such as: "I am calm, grounded, and mindful today." Around this statement, write a few things you will do to make sure it happens:

- I will meditate for ten minutes after lunch.

- I will reflect on difficult situations before I respond.

- I will practice detachment when I feel stressed.

These statements set your mind toward your goal and are already in vibrational reality once you write them. It's as if your desires are being manifested into reality because your mind is being told to shape your actions to achieve them. Writing down your goal this way will significantly increase your chances of achieving it. When you consciously decide what you want out of your day, you are also more likely to be satisfied with the outcome.

Here are a few more tips for successful early rising:

- Plan your morning the night before, and make sure you practice good bedtime rituals to get the best sleep possible.

- Essential oils like frankincense and cinnamon can illuminate earthy and grounded emotions, while sweet orange and neroli act as pick-me-ups for a slumbering mind. Rub a few diluted drops on your pulses or get a diffuser for your home.

- Be mindful of what you need in the morning: Listen to your body as soon as you wake up. Do you need to stretch? Would some music help motivate you? Do you need some fresh air? How about a few moments of reflection and gratitude?

- Try to keep off the digital path until you have set your intentions and put your mind toward the day.

Turn routines into rituals. Positive routines, such as making your first cup of coffee or saying good morning to a loved one, can be supercharged when you add conscious awareness. So instead of performing a meaningless routine, make it a powerful, purposeful ritual. Acknowledge the enjoyment of sipping that coffee; be aware of why you love that person when you say good morning. When you allow your routine to become deeply meaningful, it creates powerful, high-vibration emotions that are stored for the rest of the day. Rituals are also a way to gain control of unconscious acts that otherwise slip under the radar, so choose a few that you can turn into self-empowered acts of consciousness.

Be mindful that it takes time to change. Some people can adopt new habits easily, while others will struggle. Try your new routine for twenty-one days and then judge its effectiveness. Give yourself a time frame to experiment and choose to see this as an adventure of self-discovery. If it doesn't work for you, you haven't lost anything, only gained valuable knowledge about how you work and deal with challenges.

By choosing how you start the day, you mold your attitude, your ability to face the world, and your perception of everyday challenges. You are free to choose your mindset and pursue your greatest goals. No mind is ever cast in stone, no mood is ever eternal, and no habit is ever stronger than the will of a determined woman.

Intuition: Free the Guidance

The final step in freeing your mind is to listen to your heart.

You analyze, plan, and strategize your life in directions you think will benefit you; you consult the internet for answers to even the most personal of questions. But if you're like many people, you rarely "feel" or intuit your way into decisions.

This is especially true in the early years of motherhood. You search for every possible reason that your children won't eat, what that weird rash is, and when to start sleep training. You open yourself to opinions from the entire spectrum of knowledge. As beneficial as this is, it's also important to spend time developing your intuition to find inner guidance and align with the wisdom of your heart.

No matter how long it has been since you last heard your intuition speak, it is still waiting patiently to be heard again. In the same way that your consciousness is eternally awake, so too is your intuition, if you just listen. Trusting your own instincts is one of the most empowering things you can do. It will lead you to decisions you never knew you were capable of and to a life you wouldn't believe existed.

Intuition lies in the center of your heart and is connected to your consciousness at the back of your mind. It is an awareness of things you can't see and feelings you can't explain. With practice, stillness, and a little trust, you can regain control of this vital navigation system and live in accordance with your higher self, connect to your inner dialogue with the universe, and be the greatest version of who you truly are.

෨෬

During my oldest child's first few weeks, I calculated feeding times and searched the internet for solutions to sleep problems. I was looking for comfort: I wanted a reason for his behavior, reassurance that it was normal, and confirmation that I wasn't the only one in this situation. I tried unsuccessfully to breastfeed for a couple of months before I gave in to the pressure to bottle-feed. Nurses, friends, and family cited my lack of experience and told me I didn't know what I was doing, but I wish I had known the power of trusting my natural instincts and silencing the noise that often comes with opinions. The truth is that no first-time mother knows what she's doing, and for the most part, everything is normal.

You are never as vulnerable as when you first navigate motherhood. You distrust your innate ability to know what is right for your child and yourself. This causes you to seek advice elsewhere. The social, societal, and cultural pressures to be a certain way, to raise children in a certain way, and to embrace the idea of perfection can burden you to the point of shattering. Never in the history of womankind have the balance and expectations of motherhood been so out of sync.

My second child, a fiery redhead with a birthmark in the middle of her forehead, was my passage back to intuition. She came into the world as a powerful manifestation of all the intuitive practices I had followed throughout my pregnancy: I set a high vibration of living, practiced morning mantras that affirmed my mothering capabilities, ate intuitively, meditated regularly, and attended prenatal yoga right up to the birthdate. I didn't look for opinions on the internet and consulted the doctor only when there was something I couldn't shake. I didn't make a birth plan. I tried to listen only to the quiet calm of my inner voice, which nudged me in the right direction throughout the birth.

As a result, I had an extraordinarily different experience with my second child. I walked home with my newborn and husband only a few hours after giving birth and never felt more in control in my life. During the first few sleepless months, I continued to listen to my intuition and kindly dismissed advice that did not resonate with me.

When I needed comfort or reassurance that I was not alone or overreacting, I wrote questions in my journal that I wanted to ask a search engine, such as "How long does your three-month-old sleep at night?" I would then answer my own question. "My baby only sleeps an hour at a time and then feeds for two. I'm so exhausted! I have another kid who wakes up as well, so right now I feel like I'm walking in treacle. Hang in there, you are not alone—it will change!" This exercise never failed to make me feel better; it even encouraged me to seek medical advice when I knew intuitively that something was wrong.

Day 13: Train your intuition with the following practices:

Practice meditation daily. Meditation strengthens your connection to your intuition. Sit with an intended question and practice quieting your mind, then see what you hear or feel. This "just knowing" feels different to everyone, but it's usually located around the heart or belly as a warm lightness. It's a feeling of certainty that your mind cannot dissemble with fear or doubt. When you connect to this place of surrender and feel the comfort it gives, you can ask questions and wait for discoveries.

Be mindful. Intuition can reside only in the present moment; it cannot echo from the past or send answers from the future. Practicing mindfulness consistently will strengthen your connection to your intuition and empower you with the gift of effective decision-making.

Journal your dreams. Dreams are powerful emanations from your subconscious mind, the portal that connects the ethereal to the physical. Sleep is necessary to repair and relax your body; it also allows your mind to make sense of your emotions. Dreams bring deep, unconscious feelings to the surface. By investigating their underlying messages, you may be able to uncover the root of your challenges.

Intuition can help you interpret your dreams. Keep your journal next to your bed; if you wake up from a dream, record anything you can remember—your feelings, the environment, other people, and whether you've had the dream before. The more details you record, the more telling and useful they will be. Regular dream journaling will give your intuition a gateway for communication and become a great source of reflection. You can also look up the meanings to your dreams in books or online and see what analysis resonates with you. Dreams are very personal, so use external explanations as a way to navigate your own intuitive meaning and provide insight into your life and your deep emotions.

Try automatic writing. Open your heart by thinking of someone you truly love. Imagine being with them and feeling a powerful emotion of openness and abundance. Once you feel the pureness of love in your heart, ask yourself a question for which you seek an answer. Give yourself five minutes to write your answer, without pausing to think or expecting your writing to be logical. Automatic writing takes practice and can feel bizarre at first, but you will be surprised at what emerges from your subconscious.

Once your time is up, scan the page and highlight the words that resonate with you. Ask yourself the question again and read the highlighted words aloud. An answer will surface, and although it might not be what you want, it will have come from your heart and not from your head.

Map your life's curves. Draw your life's events as a timeline with peaks (positive changes or events) and valleys (negative changes or events). Think about what happened at those points. Did you make a decision at a peak or valley that changed your life? Did someone or something else make the decision for you? Circle the peaks where you used your intuition, and circle dips or low points where you didn't use your intuition or had no control of the outcomes.

Very often the peaks are a result of intention and consciousness, while the dips reflect unconscious acts and the lack of intuitive guidance. How has your life been shaped by your intuition or lack thereof? Remind yourself to follow your heart and intuition when faced with challenges. By trusting your decisions, you can shape your own life.

Look for signs. Your intuition has a remarkable capability to send you messages through your awareness, so combine your mindfulness with a search for signs. At the beginning of the day, tell your mind to notice repeating patterns, favorite colors, sentimental objects; spend the day being mindful of your environment. It is with intention that the mind begins to formulate outcomes, so notice what is being brought to your attention. When you need direction in life, verbalize your desire for a sign that will help you make an important decision and see what comes up in your day. When you begin to see these signs, know that you are becoming more aligned with your higher self and your intuition. Whether you believe these signs are coming *to* you or *from* you makes little difference. Look at this exercise as a compass that will always point north.

Clean up your inner dialogue. How do you talk to yourself? Do you often criticize yourself? You may be trying to adopt a more positive outlook; remember that "I am optimistic" and "I am always grumpy about something" convey completely different messages. The first statement resonates at positive, high-vibrational frequencies while the other picks up lower, negative vibes. These vibrations, in turn, attract similar frequencies (and outcomes).

Intuition speaks within those frequencies, so if it picks up negativity it will guide you to lower-vibrational outcomes. This is why it's important to be mindful with the way you speak and label yourself, because your intuition keeps you within that range of vibration. It cannot suddenly tell you that you are an incredible being full of abundance and infinite worth if you keep believing that you are not good enough.

You may not always understand what your intuition is trying to tell you, but it will never stop trying to fulfill its sacred responsibility to guide you to your happiest, healthiest, and greatest version of life. It's up to you to listen, acknowledge, and take inspired action. The more you ignore your inner voice, the more you are chained to your reactive conditionings. The more you rely on the digital world, the more you lose your power to control and navigate your life with freedom of choice.

To rely on your intuition as heavily as you rely on your other senses, trust that you have benefitted from it before. Raise your inner dialogue to a frequency that frees you from low-vibe guidance and blind choices.

Part One

Those who cannot change their minds,
cannot change anything.

—*George B. Shaw*

YOU NOW KNOW THE INSPIRED actions to free your mind. Continue to incorporate each practice into every day, and you will find conscious choice blossoming in your once-autopiloted life. You have begun to realign the manifestation wheel with intuition, intention, and freedom, so be prepared for exquisite opportunities. These signs manifest only to those with open eyes who are willing to dismantle logic with heart.

When you spend your life striving to change, attain, and satisfy surface desires through external validation, you will never be truly free. No matter what you want in life, no matter how much you deserve it, you will never truly enjoy it until you have done the necessary inner work.

When you dig into the soil of your soul and connect to your roots, you start to manifest the life that benefits you most. You start to see your problems as deceptive and often exaggerated by your state of mind. By detaching and engaging with more wholesome thoughts and actions, you resonate with higher waves of vibration. This is your highest aspiration, the universal language of love and abundance. Once you see this truth, you can nourish the desires and needs that allow you to feel contentment, joy, love, empowerment, and freedom; you release everything that does not serve you. You face your fears and demolish them with consciousness and compassion.

Instead of striving you begin to allow. Instead of resisting you start to flow. You let go of the black holes and vortices that consume your energy. Because you are infinitely inspired by what you have learned, you begin to create instead of search. Your life becomes an exciting journey of discovery, of inner wanderlust, and this new humbling perspective allows you to see how small your mind has been. Once you incorporate mindfulness into your everyday life, your mental bandwidth grows tenfold. You realize that now is all you have ever had and ever will have.

Your quest for knowledge begins with the discovery of yourself. By using this book to inspire and free your mind, you may discover parts of yourself that no longer fit who you want to become or unearth elements of yourself that you have suppressed. Perhaps your job no longer fulfills you; perhaps your friends no longer inspire you; perhaps the place you live no longer nourishes you. Perhaps you need to question how much of your life is there by consent and confront anything that exists without your intent. This is the sacred work of intentional living. If you dare to ask these difficult questions, you may be able to glimpse the exceptional life that lies before you. You may not believe such a life exists or that it could be yours, but I guarantee you that it does and that you are the only person able to create it.

In parts two and three of this book, you will discover freedom through intentional living and breaking down your comfort zone. I will help you redesign your life in alignment with your inner compass, teach you to create financial freedom, find soul-driven purpose, and live a high-vibrational life that supports your journey toward the best version of your life. Your final freedom will be to discover the art of exponential growth through adventure, which will allow you to sever the final cords that have confined you to an illusion of comfort. When you finish this book there will be no area of your life that has not been unraveled, disentangled, or released from the norms and values of your prior conditionings.

Ultimate freedom means empowering every corner of your life with your own creative and nourishing hands. This is your mutiny against the old habits that have captained your life for far too long.

Get ready to take the wheel of a life that is beyond your imagination.

PART TWO
FREEDOM OF LIFE

CHAPTER 6
Intentional Living

The authentic self is the soul made visible.

—*Sarah Ban Breathnach*

THE SECOND PART OF THIS book is a guide to designing an intentional life, one that is aligned with your rules, values, and unique blueprint. In these pages, you will not only discover practical tools, but the vibrational frequency you need in order to create a life you love, full of choice, adventure, unbridled energy, and opportunity.

As you make foundational changes to your inner world, however, your outer life may seem suddenly out of place as illusions are chipped away and raw truth emerges. Your task is to take this insight—this truth—and use it to create a potent, intentional life defined by your own rules, aligned with your inner compass, and untethered from your conditionings or others' expectations. This can be a beautiful, messy, soul-digging process.

Removing toxic relationships and negative energies are first on the to-do list. Next is changing the way you live by decluttering your home. If you live with redundant material goods and maintain toxic relationships, you cannot live your life to its highest potential. The conditions of your mind are manifested in your living conditions. The more you create flow and openness in your inner world, the more your external world will reflect this transformation.

As you continue the daily practices from Part One to create inner flow, guidance, and freedom, you will empower yourself with focus, energy, and certainty. Keep practicing until you incorporate all of the inspired actions every day. When that happens, you will have made incredible progress. From then on, the work will become a state of being and you will have gained the power to consciously transform any area of your life.

You are now ready to build your life on the foundation of true freedom, guided by soul and marked with limitless potential. Begin by asking yourself deep questions about your life, family, work environment, what you believe in, what you teach your children, and what you want to contribute to the world. It may take some rebellion, it may take some anarchy, but that's what self-empowerment is: taking back the control that already belongs to you.

CHAPTER 7
Align and Redefine Your Life

*Owning our story and loving ourselves through that process
is the bravest thing that we will ever do.*

—*Brené Brown*

I WAS WORKING FOR A fashion label in Scandinavia when I came to realize how little I had consciously intended in my life. My job, the way I lived, and how I spent my time did not support who I wanted to be. I kept hearing that you can have it all. You can have a sucessful career *and* be a dedicated mother. You can spend more time with your children *and* work over-time to pay for the cost of living. You can own a beautiful house *and* travel. I believed I could have anything if I worked hard enough at it and conformed to the way of life in Denmark.

For years I tried to earn more money so I could afford to "have it all". I changed my perspective about my job, stopped complaining, and ran harder. I focused on doing what was expected, even though it gave me migraines and severe anxiety. It made me grow deeply inward toward the exquisite abyss, and whenever I touched the void, I heard a voice telling me that a good life flows with ease and inspiration, not with constant fight, turmoil and resistance. Finally, I came to a point where I could no longer live the "have it all" life.

It took a year to change my work and living environment; this took resilience, planning, support, adjustments, flow, learning, space, and consistent motion. As I was going through this process, four of my closest friends—each of whom had at least two children and worked full-time—found that they couldn't keep up with the "having it all" life anymore and were either on prolonged sick leave or in therapy. Even in Denmark, a country famous for its work-life balance, it is difficult for a parent to stay home with their children and maintain a decent standard of living because the country's economy is built on two full-time salaries per family. I began to look for a way to be a devoted mother but still earn some type of income.

I had four compelling goals:

- First, I wanted time for myself, my husband, and my children, to nurture, grow, and be present.

- Second, I wanted to be passionate about the way I earned an income. I wanted to create, every day. I didn't want to be confined to a desk job where I had to do what I was told and contribute to someone else's bottom line. I wanted to be inspired, challenged, and engaged with interesting people. Most of all, I wanted to be in a field of work that allowed me to grow spiritually.

- Third, I wanted to live in nature, to be surrounded by its calming perspective and influence, but I also wanted to be connected to like-minded people in the city.

- And finally, I wanted to travel. It is my personal freedom, and it is when I feel I most belong.

I sincerely and unashamedly wanted my own version of "having it all."

I began to drive myself toward what felt good and quashed the guilt that usually bubbled up when I prioritized myself. I quit my job. I gave myself six months to write a book, sign with a publisher, and start writing the next one. If this plan didn't work, I would go back to my old degrading job and give up on my dreams. My husband thought this was reasonable, so he set a manifestation timeline for himself as well. He said if he couldn't find a job in his dream industry of renewable energy and get a raise so he could support me, he too would give up and settle down. To seal the deal, we planned a trip to Sri Lanka at the end of those six months, although we didn't know whether we'd be celebrating or mourning the results of our individual experiments.

No pressure.

I began my inner work with gusto. I embraced myself, the person I had become after motherhood, and decided who I wanted to be in the future. I "wore" this statement with confidence every day. I breathed it, I lived like it was already mine, but I never put it on a pedestal because I was truly grateful for everything I already had. I tweaked my living and social environment, my consumer habits, my diet, my thoughts to those that supported, encouraged, and empowered me.

I stopped trying to fit in. I stopped worrying about what people thought and started to redefine myself. I spent every waking moment learning what I needed to know to get where I wanted to be. I reconditioned my subconscious to believe I was capable of unimaginable things, and soon that became the driving force for my everyday routine. I used challenges as opportunities to separate myself from mediocrity. I applied this mindset to everything: my running, my emotions, my business plans. I became more authentically me than ever before, and I saw my superpowers were not in fact embedded in my university degree, my training certificates, or my résumé—but in my uniqueness, my originality, and my ability to do things differently. I literally redesigned myself, and at the same time, came back to the wholeness of my being. It was with this reinvention that I knew the same cycle of manifestation, the same repeating themes of the past, could simply not occur again because I, the manifestor, was incomparably different.

Unfortunately, this dramatic shift was not financially feasible with our current expenses, even for six months. Copenhagen is among the world's most expensive cities, and what we were doing was unheard of. So we made dramatic cuts, trimmed expenses, let go, simplified, and downsized our lives into a one-in, one-out lifestyle. We sold 70 percent of our material items and put the money into a savings account for our travels. Instead of giving up our freedom to pay off a mortgage, we sold our home and moved into a commune apartment with shared expenses. We also took a small part of the remaining funds and bought a piece of land on the northwest coast of Denmark, where we built a little cabin by hand. Our lives were split between the vibrancy of city life and the calmness of wilderness living. We applied conscious intention to every choice and every sacrifice, aligning our lives to the beauty of often-neglected in-between moments, which suddenly filled our days with an abundance of quality time.

There were many times that we were "encouraged" to do what was normal, to go with the grain, but by sticking to our beliefs, terms, and conditions, we created confidence in our own definition of freedom. We faced incredible pressure to buy a bigger house now that we had two kids, to work our way up in our careers because we had responsibilities, to fill our homes with digital entertainment because kids need stimulation—but that suddenly felt like a prehistoric model of living. Instead, we underwent an evolution of some kind. Choosing our slow-brewed life projected us into a deeply meaningful existence, one that we refined with our own hands.

The day we packed up to head off to Asia for a month was my husband's last day in his old job. He would return to work at the world's most influential renewable energy company. The time I'd had to be with the kids, to take sick days without a debate, to create slow-cooked meals, a happy home, and work on something profoundly meaningful meant he'd had the time to focus on his own career development.

When former colleagues heard about my rebellion, their Scandinavian "feminism" said that I was being subdued into a domestic role that was unequal to my husband's. It was funny to hear these statements, because I believe feminism is about equal worth, and not equality as in sameness. As I watched them become overstressed, overworked, and unbalanced but "equal" mothers, I signed with a publisher and returned from our travels with my dreams neatly folded into the seams of my soul.

Needless to say, our intentional manifestation resulted in an exceptional outcome. It was not easy, simple, or straightforward; it required constant adjustment, letting go, and re-creation. Aligning life with inner certainty requires resilience to face the opinions and judgments of others. But when you are a mother this is nothing new. Every time you choose to let a challenge become an opportunity to separate yourself from mediocrity, you gain traction toward the fulfillment of your dreams. Now when you look back at your past ideas, the sparks of passion you once had for a topic, a study, a business idea, an unconventional creation, a hobby, an alternative career ... perhaps you can see that you perceived challenges more as judgments, shouldn't-dos, ought-not-to-dos, or put-downs and personal criticisms—when they were really chances to become exceptional.

It is a rebellious act to drive your life from your heart rather than from your head, but it is an authentic way to live. It's infinitely better than skimming the choppy waters of conformity.

Knowing what you truly want in life is the first real challenge. Your definitions of freedom and a successful life are as unique as you are. Aligning with your intuition will lead you to your greatest version of life. It will give you the power of conviction, clarity, and insight so you can discover who you really are and map out your actions.

To get started, you'll need your journal and pen.

Envision Your Best Life

Set aside thirty minutes one day when you can relax and be in a meditative state of mind. Choose a time of day when your mind is clear and hasn't been affected by too much external information.

Spend a couple moments relaxing, taking a few deep inhalations. Feel what you need in this moment to make you completely at ease. Some meditation music, a hot drink, or a moment outside? Choose things that resonate with you individually, not what you have read that others do, and encourage your senses into a calm state of mind.

In your journal, describe a day in your best life. Use as many descriptive words as you can to connect with feelings of ease, joy, empowerment, and freedom. Be as specific as you can about your emotions, especially your feelings about yourself and your environment. What do you do in this best life that makes you feel so good? How do you behave with your children? How do you respond to your partner? Let yourself be fully immersed in this experience and allow yourself to feel the most joyous emotions and fulfillment you can imagine.

If an image arises that makes you feel something is lacking, or triggers something that you long for with desperation, think about why you feel this way. What in your life has caused you to have a difficult relationship with this object or emotion? What can you do to change your perception of it?

Perhaps the feeling of blissful love makes you feel unworthy, or the thought of a dream house by the ocean makes you feel undeserving. When this feeling of sadness, lack, or desperation appears, it is a sign to look at what is blocking you from your own happiness.

Sometimes you must address it, and sometimes you must let it go. Your intuition will know which path you must take, which action will lead to liberation. If it feels cleansing to let it go, then do that. If it keeps churning in you and comes up in other areas of your life, address it.

Identify Your Core Emotions

When you have finished this description of your day, identify the emotions you felt during this visualization. Bring your awareness only to your emotional state, not to objects or material items. Circle the emotional words you have used and write these emotions down in present tense with the powerful affirmation, "I am": I am free, I am confident, I am at ease, I am connected. You will discover how you want to feel in your best version of life, and which emotions you want to take with you into the future.

If you were to do this with a group, you would soon discover that there is not much that separates us as women. Joy, love, ease, empowerment, freedom—we all seek these, despite the immense differences between us as individuals.

Once you have this powerful list of core emotions, you can use them as an invaluable guidance system. We will be using this throughout Part Two, so keep them nearby as you continue to read. This list is the key to your intentional life.

Redefine Your Life

Your unconscious mind drives your everyday life. As you repeat the same routines, the same patterns, and the same actions, they become programmed into your subconscious. Society, culture, and the collective consensus run better and more profitably on doubt and fear than they do on joy and empowerment, so we tend to find friendships in hate, and develop a need to be justified by others. But you can break the cycle with conscious awareness of your own beautiful uniqueness.

Redefining your life starts by looking at how you live right now and noticing the differences between your current reality and your best life. This is not a comparison of what you do or don't have, but of the emotions you experience. How does your daily life compare to the positive and empowering feelings you experienced in your dream life? What core emotions are missing from your everyday living?

Align with Your Core Emotions

With every core emotion you identified, think about how often you feel it. Remember, this is not a judgment; it is simply a neutral observation that will help you map your current mindset.

- If one of your core emotions is "gratitude," for example, do you practice gratitude each day for what you have, both the good and the challenging parts?

- If you identified "excitement," do you feel excited about something in your life at the moment?

- If you wrote down "ease," do you currently go through your day with the weightlessness of ease?

For every positive core emotion you identified in your best life, parallel it with an action that will make you feel that way right now. Make it a priority to connect with at least one of your core emotions every day through meditation or journaling.

- If you wrote "I am connected," for example, your action could be "I will meditate every day for at least ten minutes and create an inner connection with myself."

- "I am at ease" could be activated by "I will practice detachment and letting go of the things that make me stressed."

Create a physical or digital vision board using different images, quotations, and colors that resonate with your heart and your vision of your best life. Add photos of your family, your loved ones, and pictures that make you feel most alive. Make a sacred space where you can reflect on these images, gain perspective, inspire action, and access your core emotions on a daily basis.

Fuel Your Intentional Life

Now that you have identified your core emotions and discovered a way to access them, you will use them to fuel an intentional life. Since emotions direct outcomes, drive your life with high-vibration emotions—love, excitement, joy, empowerment, gratitude, and freedom. You probably identified many of these as core emotions in the best version of your life.

The more you tap into these emotions and focus on actions that create them, the more you empower your life. You not only become the mistress of your own happiness, but you are also in the receiving mode that attracts emotional, physical, financial, and spiritual wealth.

Let Go

It's important to realize that some elements of life are not aligned with your core emotions and that you need to let them go. Situations, people, and activities that do not resonate with your core emotions do not serve you. Intentional living means that you must adjust, tweak, dig, question, step back, say no (or yes), and embody your core emotions every single day in the life you have right now. As you do, you will begin to see your life transforming into something quite remarkable.

If you forget these core emotions you will start letting feelings of "lack" slip in again: the things that would make your life so much easier, the love that would make you so much happier, the freedom that would make you more content, the confidence that would make you feel so much more worthy. Lack breeds lack, so when you are in a "lacking" state of mind you must make it a priority to come back to yourself, to connect to your core emotions, and focus on your inner work. Only abundance can lead to more abundance, so take the time to acknowlege the good in your life, in what you have, and in who you are.

Once you have identified your core emotions, it is time to let go of the specifics of your "dream life"—the car you would drive, the house you would live in, the clothes you would wear. As much as you aspire to those things, you will never be satisfied by them until you have done the groundwork that makes you feel unconditionally joyful about life.

Always remember this: You will *always* desire more. Even when you have the tangible manifestation in your hands, your life will always offer contrast and ask you to grow more. What you wanted ten years ago is different from what you want now, so accept the feeling of consistent desire as directional, not as discontenting.

Like all humans, you have three stages of consciousness; you continuously shift in and out of them. In the first stage, you feel out of control and have little joy; you live in fear, disappointment, and lack. In the second stage, you learn more about how you can get through a situation; this is when you are inspired to act. The third and highest stage of consciousness is when you let go of outcomes, expectations, and control. Here you meet the universe with your heart open to all that the mind cannot rationalize. You go through these stages on a continual basis, and the more you align with yourself, the more time you spend navigating between the second and third stages of consciousness.

Alignment is simply the intersection of your best self and the person you are right now. Defining the emotions of who you want to be is your core work; realigning your life every day to meet these emotions is the foundation on which you can build an intentional life. Creating an intentional life means knowing what you want, then letting go of everything that does not support it.

When you consciously intend to be the best version of yourself, you become it. Knowing your core emotions and incorporating more activities that access them will align your life with what is really important. You may find yourself doing more of what you love because it is one of the best ways to access your passionate self. By repeating your self-empowering statement every morning, you recondition your belief system to one that is nourishing and open to abundance. Alignment is truly empowering.

Write a Self-Empowering Statement

Others may have defined you in the past, but now you will define yourself with resolve and intent by writing a statement that reflects your vision of your best self. Read it every morning as a positive affirmation exercise and embody it as often as you can throughout the day. Watch your life shift as you commit to this practice, especially when you deal with challenges. This will transform the way you see yourself and the way that others interact with you.

When you write a self-empowering statement, you catalyze a shift in your higher self. When you repeat it every morning and pull in your core emotions to this practice, you start to believe it, and once you believe it, anything is possible. The power of belief has the ability to create worlds.

Use the statement below as an inspiration and starting point, adjusting it to your own desires and core beliefs. Give yourself permission to feel that you are truly worthy of these words.

> *I am empowered by my intent and confident in my choices. My actions are guided by my intuition and I am connected to my inner source of knowing. I am grounded. The roots within me are deep, interlacing with all that I truly am. This allows me to grow tall, strong, and resilient.*
>
> *I have an infinite ability to love, and I bring this power into the world with compassion, openness, and a desire to share it. I live a high-vibrational and abundant life because I know that I am the conscious creator of all that I have. Everything in my existence is a reflection of my beliefs, emotions, and actions.*
>
> *I am aligned with my higher self, the best version of who I truly am, and I am committed to discovering what makes me vibrant and passionate. I am deeply grateful for all that I have, and I surrender to the universe with an open heart. I am nourished, I am free, and I am guided by a connection to my source energy. I am open to receiving guidance and trust the gift of divine timing.*
>
> *May I be met with the knowledge and opportunities that I seek. May I walk this day in the light of my highest self, and may I take the time to consciously shift toward the actions that allow me to access my core emotions and their limitless inspiration.*

As you realize what aligns with your core emotions (and what does not), you become inspired to take action. You do more of what you love and what feels good, and you let go of anything that does not serve your highest self. You might try out an idea you've been harboring for years. Perhaps you'd like to change your job, social group, hobbies, or home. Perhaps you'll redefine the goals you've been striving toward so that you can spend more time in nature or nourish your soul with a group of inspiring people.

The need for soul alignment can come gradually, like the blossoming of flowers in spring, or it may come in as a hard winter, shedding the life that covers its core. Whatever changes you decide are necessary, remember that while you remain a spiritually limitless being, your children and spouse will be affected by every choice you make. You will need to ease out of your old life before you shift into a new one.

Freedom does not mean having limitless choices. True freedom is the ability to choose within limitations. These limitations are not restrictions—rather, they are parameters that provide an area in which freedom can truly flourish. Numerous psychological studies show that when we are faced with too many choices, we become significantly more depressed, more stressed, and less satisfied. To know your parameters is to know true freedom.

When you align with more of what you want in life and less of what you don't, you start to create your parameters. When you create them with intent, they become guides that liberate you from that vast, barren landscape of possibility. Parameters are essential supports for intentional living, and they provide a potent area for growth.

Defining your parameters is the opposite of living blindly with assumed limitations. It turns sacrifices into choices and allows every aspect of your life to be ruled by consciousness.

Choose Your Parameters

Use a few pages in your journal to map your parameters.

On the first page, write down all the goals you have in life. Leave a couple lines after each so you are able to add comments. The goals can be anything specific, e.g., financial freedom, a new house, a new job, more friends, more time. Dig deep and tap into some of the feelings you felt as you aligned with your core emotions.

Under each goal, write down anything that keeps you from attaining it.

- Is it a psychological, social, or financial limit? For example, maybe your dream is to work for yourself and earn your own income. A psychological limitation might be that you're not sure if you have the emotional resilience to run a business. A financial limitation might be that you do not have enough disposable income to invest in your idea right now. A social limitation might be that you do not have a network or online platform yet.

- For each limitation, ask yourself, "Can I change this limit?" If not, ask, "How can I change my attitude about this limit?" To go back to the above example, you could combat your psychological fear of not being emotionally resilient enough by changing your mindset through physical exercise and meditation. The financial limit might be changed by selling unused household items or researching how to start a business with little to no start-up costs. The social limitation can be overcome by taking a free confidence course online, socializing more within your existing network, and treating interactions with new people as opportunities for collaboration.

- If you can change the limit, ask yourself, "What am I willing to give up for this goal?" Ask yourself if you are willing to give up a few hours a week to research your business idea. Will you be able to overcome your social fear in order to network and attend events? Are you willing to work from home and be disciplined with your time? Can you give up negative self-talk in favor of conditioning your mind to your success?

- If you cannot change the limit because the price is too high, then it is time to change your attitude toward what you want and embrace the parameter. If you are a highly sensitive person and know that networking would drain your energy, you can adjust your mindset to one of acceptance and move on to ideas that don't involve networking. If you are unable to give up a few hours a week to research your business, perhaps now is not the time for self-empolyment; instead, work on allowing more time in your life to do what you love.

By the time you have completed this task for all of your goals, you will notice that some things can be left alone while others require action. When you decide what is worth giving up, then you have consciously determined a desire that is worthy of your attention. As you realign and define your life you will notice that what you say yes and no to reinforces your parameters. Be mindful of how you use them because as simple as they are, they determine your life.

Remember to recognize the beauty in your limitations and embrace the reason they are there. Changing your attitude toward the things you cannot change means taking control of your life. Accepting parameters rather than complaining about sacrifices gives you vital control. While it's tempting to assume that limits are beyond your control, perhaps the truth is that you are not willing to give up what is required to attain what you want. This allows you to be grounded in your choices and take responsibility for them.

෬෬

For a long time, I wanted to live in a rural, isolated part of the world where I would be submerged in nature. It ticked every box of my core emotions. When I brought up the subject to my husband (who also grew up on a farm), he said that he too dreamed about getting back to the simplicity of nature.

Then, in a divine sign from the universe, I received an email from a friend in central Portugal who asked if we wanted to come stay with them and help build a yurt that they needed to put up for a summer retreat. My husband and I saw this as the chance we needed to get some insight into that kind of life. So, that winter, we traveled with our two young children to the mountains of Portugal's Centro region for the experiment of a lifetime.

We lived in a safari tent on their large property, next to a river. It had a small, inefficient wood burner that kept us on our toes when it snowed and the temperatures dropped below zero. We spent our days exploring the valley, helping out with the farm chores and reacquainting ourselves with the rewards and exhaustion of manual labor. Part of the experiment was to see if we could truly live there, so we also searched for run-down villas in the area that we could rennovate.

This was life in its rawest form, and it challenged me to the brink of my comfort zone. Hardship and reward were constantly shifting. We created and fixed things daily and spent quality time together (albeit in survival mode), which bonded us incredibly. At the end of our time, we had to make a decision: to go back to our life in Denmark or stay in Portugal.

Our friends encouraged us to buy the farm next door. They said that it was the best life we would ever know. We believed them, but there was one limitation that held me back.

Throughout the stay, I journaled my feelings and kept track of how often my core emotions came into play. But one issue kept coming up, and it was intuitive: I felt I would have to sacrifice my children's well-being to make this dream come true. They would either have to attend the one and only local school or we would have to homeschool them and balance their education with our work to create an income from the villa, which would require all our time to renovate. We were accustomed to the hardship that comes with that type of work, thanks to our experience building our cabin in Denmark, but we knew that when a project becomes the means to food on your table, it loses its romance. I acknowledged this limit and that I would not sacrifice to change it. This caused undeniable sadness on our journey home.

A few weeks later, I received a call from the friend with whom we'd stayed. She no longer felt inspired by her husband and had escaped dramatically one night with a man who had come to stay at her retreat. Through a messy, soul-destroying process, she ran away from her family in search of herself. I reflected deeply on this difficult news, but it validated my refusal to make the sacrifice that would have been required. In fact, that limitation stopped us from making what could have been a very regrettable decision. As a result, one of my parameters for an extraordinary life now includes what I am *not* willing to sacrifice.

This episode was also the first time I encountered something I've seen in many of our experimental travels—women who choose "freedom" over children. Over the years we have stayed in off-grid communities in the mountains, tiny beach shacks on deserted islands, yurts in national parks, and wooden cabins in isolated forests. In these travels, I have met a few women who live unconventionally and have relative freedom, but have yet to untether themselves from themselves. Motherhood can impose a physical restriction, but the choice of spiritual liberation is always at hand. It's those of us who have woven motherhood into the warp and weft of our womanhood that wear the true fabric of freedom.

Change Your Perception of Wealth

We all have beliefs and attitudes about money that have been imprinted on us from an early age. How much you have—whether it's an abundance or just enough to get by—is determined to a great extent by these beliefs. How you spend and invest your money also says a lot about who you are and what you believe.

With a few changes in your perceptions, you can start to invest in things that will help you live your best life—one that affords you a little extra pocket money, a little more sunshine, a few more choices and options.

Your first task is to understand how your beliefs determine your wealth. This is especially important for women, because we are notorious for undervaluing ourselves. I might believe that money is the root of all evil, whereas you may believe that money gives people the ability to help others. Whatever beliefs you link with money either hold you back from or propel you toward financial abundance. Whether you grew up around words of financial scarcity, like, "There's not enough money for that," or if you were raised in a household that never worried about having enough money, you will likely carry those beliefs and mentalities into adulthood. Women are often subconsciously taught that money is a masculine-only energy. Therefore, they are less likely to ask for raises at work, demand better benefits in their employment contracts, or get funding for their start-ups. Money is simply energy; whether you attract more or less of that energy depends on your mindset.

To condition your mind to seek financial opportunities, you need to link the certainty of pain with a lack of money and link a certainty of pleasure to its abundance.

You will need your journal and ten minutes to think clearly. You will be asked to access some early memories and dream a little, so grab a hot drink or a glass of wine to help make this a fun exercise and lighten the mood that often comes with thinking about money.

1. Write down all the pain you experience because you don't have the financial abundance you want.

    *   Do you miss out on activities?

- Are there things you want but can't have?

- Are there people you're not able to help?

Associate this pain with the lack of money. Really feel how the lack of financial freedom burdens you and your ability to live the best version of your life.

2. What does "lots of money" mean to you?

- Do people with "lots of money" make you envious?

- Do you feel "lots of money" will ultimately create unhappiness?

- Do you feel like you deserve "lots of money"?

The questions above will help you identify your associations with financial abundance: negative, positive, or neutral.

3. What negative comments about money did your parents or family make? For example:

- Money doesn't grow on trees.

- Money is the root of all evil.

- No one gets paid to do what they love.

- If you have more than you need, you'll become greedy.

This question will help you become aware of how money was perceived in your household, whether you had to work your heart out to get a few pennies or you had everything given to you without having to work for it.

Take a look at questions two and three. While you probably like the idea of "lots of money," you may have been taught that "too much will make you greedy." Phrases like these are triggers that can cause you to react in a certain way. If you associate "lots of money" with "greedy," you actually inhibit your ability to gain wealth with a belief that may not even be yours.

You must loosen and disarm these triggers so that they do not determine your life.

If you were taught that you could never be paid well for doing something you love, maybe you now have an unfulfilling career. If you were told that money was tight, then perhaps you are just making ends meet. However, if you were taught that there is plenty of money to be had, that you deserved your share of it, and that you simply needed to play on your talents and passions to access it, then perhaps you are doing a job you love, making good money from it, and using it to benefit others.

You can begin to make this perceptual shift by associating pleasure and a better life with financial abundance, and associating pain with a lack of money, your old inherited belief systems, and your negative triggers.

4. Now write how your life would be greater, instantaneously, if you had financial abundance.

Really feel what it would be like to have so much money in your account that you could do anything, help anyone, afford anything, go anywhere. Think about the positivity, power, and options you would have.

5. Go through each limiting or negative belief that you wrote down and change the belief by attaching a new perception to it.

For example, if you wrote, "I was taught that money is the root of all evil," change it to "Money is the root of all *choice*. It gives me the option to help others, to grow in my own life, to expand beyond my circumstances. There is plenty of money flowing through the world and I deserve a portion of it. My dreams and desires are worthy and my ability to help others will extend to my family as well as strangers. I am grateful for all I have that allows me to live this life; an abundance of money will give me a freedom that I can share with others."

Read this every evening before bed and as you wake each morning until the negative triggers no longer have the power to control your life.

As with all high-vibrational desires that align with the universe, it's important to abide by a few wholesome and intuitive rules to ensure the most sustainable outcome:

- Genuinely acknowledge your appreciation for everything in your life. Gratitude is the universal language of abundance.

- Give more to others, even if it isn't a lot. Most people say they will give more when they have more, but what you do now with what you have now is a habit you will take with you on your journey to financial wealth.

- Always give without expecting to receive.

- Focus on exceeding, not on "just getting by." That mindset does not serve you or your family. "Just getting by" is like burying your potential under a heap of limitations. Your purpose in this life is not to simply endure. Your purpose is to thrive, to build, and to make your short time here inspiring to those who follow.

By this point you may be ready to say, "Okay, great. But what next?" You can do the foundational work to change your perceptions, but that in itself will not provide you with financial abundance. You need a vessel (a job, a trade, a passion) to tap into the flow of money.

As you clear your inner roadblocks, you will open a path for inspiration that will guide you to a vessel. Your inspired vessel will come by combining your skills, your passions, and, most importantly, your ability to seek new opportunities.

To align with these vessels is to seek with open eyes and see the world as an infinite array of possibilities. If you believe you have "missed your boat" or that chances only come "once in a blue moon," then you have closed your eyes. Good opportunities are alignments waiting to happen, and the best way to become more aware of them is to start realizing that you must see them to embrace them.

Here is a story that illustrates how seeing the same thing differently can help you align with a vessel of opportunity.

> You're standing on a beach, looking down at your feet. You are searching for shells but can only find one or two. You start to panic and search harder. You came to the beach to find as many shells as you could, and you don't want to disappoint anyone.

You continue to look only in the area around your feet. Your perimeter is only one meter in any direction. For some unknown reason, you believe shells only gather where your feet press down on the soft sand. Someone taught you this—perhaps it was your mother or maybe your culture.

Suddenly, you ask yourself: "Does that make sense?" This question jolts everything out of perspective. You shift your gaze beyond your toes and look further along the shore. Now you see hundreds of shells glinting on the beach. There are so many you can't count them; they are infinite, and they are yours to use however you wish.

It doesn't matter what you once believed, because now you can see the truth with your own eyes—and that is all that matters from here on out.

Your formula for freedom of wealth will depend on a number of factors. For example, your current financial situation, what you choose to give up, your mindset, the "vessel" that inspires you toward sustainable wealth, and the consciousness you apply to finding new opportunities—all of these can shape your journey to financial freedom. Anyone who has ever created their own abundance of wealth has been through these stages.

When you are passionate about an idea that might create financial freedom, take it as a sign of alignment with your best life. This passion drives you to create your own freedom, rather than seeking it through others' permission or a paycheck. When you feel passionate about an idea, a career shift, or working fewer hours, you must ask yourself, "What parameters am I willing to create in order to make my plan most potent?" Sifting out the sacrifices you are not willing to make is how you ensure that your plan will be successful.

Give yourself permission to try earning your own money if you believe it will provide you with more freedom. If you want to start a business, give yourself a time frame to see if it can work. Remember: A dream with a deadline becomes a goal, a goal broken down into incremental steps is a plan, and a plan backed by inspired action becomes a manifested reality.

Some people's passions ignite under pressure; they tend to be more resourceful and open to risk. Others prefer to slow-simmer ideas, sift out variables, and work from a place of security. Whichever category you fall into, make sure you break your vision into daily, achievable steps. What knowledge, time, finances, resources, and mindset do you need to get your idea off the ground?

What are you willing to give up to achieve this goal? If you won't give up your evenings to do the research needed or won't change your spending habits so you can save money, then perhaps this is not the right time.

Creating a vessel that leads to financial abundance requires work, but when your efforts benefit your family and not your boss, it never feels like the same struggle. Working consistently, learning new skills, adjusting your idea, and networking are all challenges, but don't let that deter you. The more aligned you are with yourself, your goals, and your dreams, the easier it is to take the right actions that lead to success. Even when you feel like you are doing what so many others are doing, remember that there is no one else in the world like you, and that your uniqueness is what will make your message different.

Working harder means working smarter, learning more, and using the infinite knowledge of the internet to your advantage. There are billions of people in the world and many of them are waiting to invest in an idea like yours, and the more unique, abstract, and specialized the service or product, the greater its chance of success. Everyone is searching for something to make life easier and more fulfilling; perhaps your idea could contribute to the growth of consciousness and connection.

To assess your path to financial independence, it's vital that you have a transparent awareness of your spending habits. Realize that *not* spending is just as important as earning income and reframe your expenditures as *investments*. Investments that nourish, sustain, and tend to your well-being will create an abundance of wealth. If you invest in nutritious food, your body will benefit. Investing in online TV subscriptions, alcohol, cigarettes, or drugs will not sustain an intentional life. Vices like these undermine true experiences and simple pleasures.

∂∆

When we looked at our finances to see if we could afford our six-month experiment, we saw that it was not possible without some extensive changes.

So we downsized. Now, in our tiny loft apartment in the city, we have to navigate tantrums, homework, playtime, worktime, and bedtimes. There are only two doors, and nowhere to hide. Little spats, annoyances, and arguments have to get ironed out immediately. After school, the kids get the floor space, which means no one can work. Although the apartment is crowded, our hand-built cabin in the wilderness gives us a place of retreat.

We also downsized our wardrobes and the kids' toys. Once a month we swap one large bag of used toys for another bag of used toys, and the kids get to discover an entirely new set of games. We got rid of the TV. We spend almost all our time outdoors in parks, museums, and at the playground.

This way of living has opened the door to freedom in a whole new way. As we grow and come to the inevitable need for more room, I know I will look back at this time as one of true inner growth and splendor, because we needed so little and experienced so much. What we considered a downsize at first has in fact been an upgrade—one that gave us the freedom to find our purpose. This helped us find the aligned vessels that will carry us toward financial, emotional, and physiological freedom in the future.

Find your financial freedom

- Work through your relationship with money and perceptions of financial wealth. Get rid of any negative associations you have with wealth by reconditioning your mind to associate pain with a lack of money, and pleasure with abundance.

- Live in a state of wealth by giving to those in need, showing your gratitude for everything you have, and knowing that you already have everything you need to flourish.

- Know that there are three roads to financial independence:

  - Earn more money by getting a better-paying job.

  - Spend less by cutting your expenditures.

  - Invest the wealth you already have into making more money.

- Review your financial options with an accountant. Learn how your money is made, spent, and invested to create better growth.

- Downsize your life to increase your freedom. Are there major expenditures that prevent you from making beneficial choices?

- If you want complete financial independence, consider starting your own business. Use your skills, passions, and knowledge to provide others with something that betters their lives and creates value.

- Create a plan for your dream—one that comes from choosing to give up another part of your time. Make it incremental and achievable. Motivate yourself by having a plan for every possibility until you gain your footing on the road that will lead most sustainably to your goal.

- Motivate and support your partner or spouse by reminding them that financial freedom will benefit the whole family. Communicate your dreams and ideas to ensure the success of your goals. Stay clear and focused to support each other. Co-creating your life with your partner is the quickest way to manifesting your best life, because it holds the power of two creative energies.

- See your path to financial freedom as a maze, one that has inevitable blocks. These are diversions that require you to turn around, work smarter, and keep going. Believe that you will achieve this goal and let your focus become a vortex for all the opportunities that will support you. Don't conform to how others' have built their businesses, but be willing to do things your own way, using your own intuition. That way, you will make your success so inevitable that no obstacle will be able to stop you.

CHAPTER 8
Create Your Purpose

The purpose of freedom is to create it for others.

—*Nelson Mandela*

IN MY EARLY DAYS, I gave little thought to my purpose in life. I moved with the tide, the moon cycle, or a passing comment about a new destination. I had a career in fashion and marketing that sent me all over the world, but I never felt that work was my purpose. It was simply a means to an experience—and always short term.

Once I became a mother, I decided my purpose would be to care for my child, to create a childhood that resonated with my own, and to be there for him while he was young. I dedicated myself to this role with every fiber of my being, and my soul responded by awakening new meaning in my life. But a few years and a second child later, I had an unsettling realization that popped up like a cork no matter how much I resisted it.

I realized that when you make your purpose in life a "someone," you are constantly required to change for them. Changing yourself for yourself, on the other hand, is incredibly liberating, inspiring, and self-empowering.

Motherhood touched every corner of my life in the most transformative way, but it did not satisfy my need for personal growth, intuitive connection, or individualism. Being a dedicated mother is not the same as finding purpose in that role. You can be a dedicated employee, wife, partner, and daughter—but you are not defined by these roles, either. Your purpose in life is not a singular something. If it were, how could you adjust to the seasonal changes in your life, the person you eventually become, the partner you choose, the children you create? Your purpose in life is, in fact, dynamic and creative.

You put meaning and purpose into your life; *you* create the reason for your own existence. Creation is your ability to think differently, to take your unique point of view, to build something, to intentionally manifest your desires into being, to laugh, to rise, and to flourish. Creation means doing what feels good, being bold and spontaneous. Creation is a root to the earth from which all life springs, a connection to the wings of your soul. It cannot be tamed, switched off, or labeled as inferior to knowledge.

When you use your heart to create purpose, you build with a tool that has a universal origin. You can create a home, create a child, create a community, create a painting, create an experience, create a life that is your own and share it with those you love. Creation, on a daily basis, accumulates well-being that no logic can dismantle or rationalize. Creation is guided by your soul in ways that you yourself do not know. That is the beauty of creation. It has a life of its own and it goes where it feels most nourished and most free.

₭⇓

As a mother, you prioritize your dreams by how much you are willing to give up for others. What is usually sacrificed, however, is yourself. You put things off now because it is not the right time for someone else. You stay a little longer in a place that isn't good for you because you don't want to make drastic decisions. When you analyze risk, you suppress your innate desires for the benefit of stability.

By living a life that does not resonate with your highest self, however, you inadvertently teach your children a destructive lesson. How will they learn self-care if they are taught to sacrifice themselves for others? Self-care is not about manicures and hot baths (although those are lovely). It is about empowering yourself to the best of your ability so that you can inspire others. Mothers tend to be the pillars of most family structures, but you cannot support anything when you are crumbling yourself.

What does your life right now teach your children?

Intentionally manifesting your best life as a mother is undeniably challenging. It is bound to the emotional and physical needs of others and is usually negotiated with partners who have different dreams and desires. But once you can articulate what you know you want for yourself—and express it without guilt—then you know what is best for your family, too.

I know a few women who gave up on motherhood to manifest their personal dreams, and not one of them is satisfied with the outcome. If anything, the desire to separate the dreams you have as an individual from those you have as a mother causes the most pain. Parameters give you satisfaction; they force you to choose from within life's most potent areas. As a woman with strong desires and a mother with conscious parameters, intentional manifestation—creating what you want—is a recipe for an extraordinary life.

In this chapter you will learn how to manifest what you want using all the work you have done so far. Make sure you have the following written down before you start:

• What a day in your best life feels like

• Your core emotions, as identified through visualization

• How to align with your core emotions every day

• What tangible thing you want in your life right now

• Your empowerment statement

• Your current parameters and what you are willing to give up

• Your plan to overcome psychological blocks to financial freedom

• Your current purpose

Follow the guide below for each element you want to manifest into your life and keep up your foundational work from Part One as you continue to read this book. That way, while you decide how your tree will blossom, you will also be working on its roots, which will ensure that your dreams are sustainable.

Know what you want and be specific. Think about the value you are adding to the world or how you are helping people with what you want. Realize that what you want might change tomorrow and that that shouldn't garner judgment.

Use your vision board. Add images of your goal every day. Choose pictures that resonate with you and what you want your reality to look like. The images you choose should inspire and motivate you.

Make a plan. Start from the result you want and work backward. Break up the journey into steps of inspired actions. Identify one thing you can do every day that will bring you closer to what you want and write it down. Use the internet to find other people who have accomplished what you want to accomplish, then learn from and be inspired by them. Even if your progress is incremental, after a few weeks of one action a day, you will be dramatically closer to the knowledge or steps necessary to achieve your dream.

Create a positive mindset. There will be challenging moments that tempt you to give up, but trust the process. Experiment with your ability to stay motivated, maintain a high-vibrational mindset, and keep your intentional manifestation going. Many people fall at the first hurdle and give up, but make that your motivation to carry on, to be extraordinary, to be the one that succeeds. Welcome challenges as a means to separate yourself from the pack. Fill your head with books, music, podcasts, and documentaries that inspire you to keep beating the odds. The alternative is to never know your true potential and be like so many others who talked themselves out of their own awesomeness.

Practice gratitude and compassion. Acknowledge the things in your life for which you are grateful, and practice small acts of compassion whenever possible. This allows you to come from a humble, grounded place that aligns with your highest self.

Ask the universe. As co-creator of your dream, the universe can help you achieve your aspirations. You just need to ask clearly for what you want. Through meditation, prayer, or by conscious reflection on your vision board, ask the universe to give you signs, opportunities, and direction that will help you attain your goal. Acknowledging your need for help is an authentic expression of surrender, and it will trigger your subconscious to offer solutions.

Notice the signs. The universe will align opportunities for you that match your core emotions. You will see signs of this alignment as doors open, numerical patterns recur, new people come into your life, old friends return to your life, quotations and phrases stand out to you, and even spam emails trigger a connection with your goal. Document these synchronicities in your journal as evidence that you are on the right path. Anything that aligns with your goal is a sign that your need has been heard and is expanding into the universe.

Take the chance. When you feel you are being inspired to take a chance toward your goal, make the decision with your heart. Does it align with your core emotions? Does it inspire you? Does it make you feel alive? If your answer to each of these questions is "yes," then go for it. Do it before you manage to talk yourself out of it. These are the opportunities worth living intentionally for.

Adopt a high-vibrational lifestyle. Your best life will always be connected to your highest self and your ability to align with your intentions every day. You can do this with a high-vibrational lifestyle, which supports a clean, conscious, and compassionate way of living and thinking. Part One of this book has already aligned you with a high-vibrational mindset; the next chapter will connect you with the environment you need to raise your vibration and meet the universe.

Accept variations. You may believe you know exactly what you want, but when you are co-creating your life with universal factors that are beyond your control, you will need to accept variations of your dreams. Every time you align with your highest self to make a decision through meditation or intuitive decision-making, you put your dreams in the hands of the universe—and sometimes it knows better. Accept that whatever comes your way is a lesson, not evidence that manifestation doesn't work. It always works, just not always in the ways you expect. You are here to learn and to expand, so accept challenges as accelerators to your liberation. In letting go, you truly show your trust in the third level of consciousness.

Nothing is more empowering on the journey to intentional living than the discovery of who you really are and how you want to live your life. Conscious manifestation changes how you think, speak, and act. Like a bodyguard, you now determine what you will let into your life and what you won't. This allows only the most valuable, nourishing, and nurturing elements to drive you. Doing what you love feeds the flames of joy, passion, and freedom. These elements can withstand any storm and guide you to the lighthouse that resides within your soul.

Trusting in a future that you have yet to feel, touch, taste, smell, or hear is the most challenging aspect of intentional manifestation, but it is this trust of something beyond your physical senses that allows you to access the true nature of conscious creation.

The next chapter will address your collaboration with the universe, and the lifestyle shifts that will raise your vibrational energy. Let it inspire an awareness of how you currently live and embolden what now resonates within you.

CHAPTER 9

The High-Vibrational "Diet"

There is another world and it is in this one.

—*Paul Éluard*

Humans are made of cells, which are made of atoms, which are made of particles, and those so-called particles are actually just vibrating energy. Every atom is just a probability wave, and most of what we call physical matter is really made up of completely empty space.

Even your thoughts vibrate at a certain frequency, and when you are said to be in a low-vibrational state, it means you are focusing on negative thoughts, speaking to yourself critically, acting on negative emotions, living without joy, and making decisions based on fear. In this state you feel run-down; your energy is depleted and you attract only low vibrations.

In a high-vibrational state, you attract not only your core emotions but the tangible desires you are working to manifest. High-vibrational living also means having conscious awareness of what you consume in the way of food, media, friends, books, music, self-talk, and attention. It is a way of living that nurtures you, and it always prizes the sustainable nourishment of your joy over quick-fix feel-good solutions.

When I discovered high-vibrational living, it propelled me into the best version of my life I had ever known. It combined all my empowerment practices and reflected them into my physical world. It solidified, materialized, and manifested a deeply enriching life. It aligned my home, my habits, my nutrition, and my impact on the world with conscious awareness.

Yet universal laws are often misunderstood. Some people assume that simply wishing for something, as long as they truly believe it is already theirs, will make it suddenly manifest into their lives. People who hold this misguided, surface-level understanding believe it is unnecessary to work for dreams or deal with their deeply rooted, destructive conditionings, and this means that they are usually disappointed with the results of manifestation.

The law of vibration says that your collective habitual thoughts constantly manifest your life in accordance with frequencies that predict positive or negative outcomes. When you want to change your life, you need to look at the vibrational frequencies of your habits and thought patterns.

Is your vibrational life at an optimal frequency? Find out by asking yourself the following questions. Remember that few people can answer yes to all of them.

- Do you talk to yourself with compassion and kindness?

- Do you love your body and is it able to move and express itself freely?

- Is your home clear, clean, and focused on a few purposeful items?

- Do you feel you are able to replenish yourself in your home?

- Is your job meaningful and balanced with your personal life?

- Is your free time spent doing things you love, that reconnect you to a place of passion and joy?

- Are you excited about the future?

- Do you see the purpose in where you are now?

- Are you expanding your consciousness and learning more about how to live your best life?

- Do you have healthy habits that nourish your body, free your mind, and connect you to your higher self?

- Are you surrounded by inspiring people who fill your life with different perspectives?

Now that you've assessed your current condition, you're ready to start your high-vibrational "diet" using seven simple practices to raise your mind, body, and soul to meet the energetic abundance of the universe. As you do these exercises, remember to journal the elements that resonate with your core being. There is no "one size fits all" in spiritual alignment; only you can feel your way into your best life.

Raise Your Home

Your home reflects your emotional state, who you are, and the things that hold meaning in your life. Like your body, you live in your home every day. It's a place of rest, nourishment, safety, and belonging. It's your center point. Aligning your home environment with your core emotions will inspire a potent life. A home that is uplifting, inspiring, and intentional can lead to major psychological and spiritual clarity.

When we moved into our small Scandinavian apartment, I discovered a solution for my cluttered life: minimalism. Coming from a home full of excess, I never knew what impact a blank, white wall could have on my mind. My husband, by contrast, had nothing useless. Everything had a purpose, everything had a place, and everything was made of quality materials. With him as my inspiration, I even pared down what I thought were absolute necessities: I had a collection of jackets for the winter, but I realized that staying warm did not require me to own many good items, just one excellent one. And so minimalist quality became the theme of my transition from tropical soul to Nordic survivor.

Decluttering and minimalism can help you access freedom more quickly. They connect your mind, body, and soul to a high-vibe state by sifting out anything that does not serve you. They keep your life potent with meaning and quality. If you wanted to move, could you pack up your life in a weekend? Are the attic and basement in order? Could you turn on a dime to take advantage of any opportunity that arises? This is the task of alignment; to get yourself and your home in order so that when the universe opens up opportunities, you are ready without hesitation.

It takes time to detach yourself from items you "simply can't throw away"—just as it's difficult to discard certain beliefs—so start with the things that have no purpose or do not serve who you want to be in the future. Be honest with yourself, just as you practiced in Part One.

Distinguish things that have meaning and purpose from those that hold emotional baggage. Redundant items, unused things, and emotionally negative attachments keep your home in a low-vibe frequency: the items of clothing you never wear, the attic full of things that you are not even aware of anymore, the cabinet of glassware that is saved for special occasions.

With every item you give away or sell, you free yourself from excess. You create potency for the purest experiences, items, and memories that truly serve you and attract more undiluted life. As you begin to detach yourself from possessions, you will begin to place more importance on experiences. This gives a sense of lightness, ease, and freedom that becomes wholesomely addictive. It creates more awareness of how you purchase things, it saves money on impulse spending, and it creates a space where creativity and inspiration can flow.

Task: Raise vibration in your home

Follow the steps below to raise the vibration in your home and watch as your life begins to create space and spontaneity. Your goal is to create an area that inspires love, purpose, and joyful memories.

- Go through one room in your home and remove items that have no purpose, hold negative emotions, or aren't used regularly. Question the validity of everything in the room.

- When you find it emotionally difficult, remember that your household items manifest energy that affects your thoughts and emotions. By raising the vibration of your home, you are also raising your manifested life to meet its highest potential.

- Designate the items you set aside as "to give away" or "to sell." Make a plan to get them out that week and do not store them for another time. If you have an item that holds negative memories but are not yet willing to let it go, move it out of your living environment. After a month, see if you have missed it. Did its absence give you emotional freedom or cause you pain? If you thought about it often, bring it back into your home. Make a meditation practice about this item and question why you are not willing to let it go despite the negative emotions it holds.

- Fill each room with as much light as possible. Use natural light or lamps to create a calming, inspiring atmosphere.

- Clear as many surfaces as possible. Take items off the walls that you do not notice on a daily basis.

- Try to create a digital-free day, opting for board games, books, and the creativity that comes from not being able to use devices.

- After a week of working with a room, journal about the experience. If you felt a positive outcome, try it again on another room until you have sifted through your entire house and found its potency.

- Clean as you go—don't neglect clutter and messes. Spend a few moments on your home each Sunday to make sure your vibe starts high in the following week.

- Once your home makes you feel inspired and at ease, dedicate a blank wall to your future. Make it a family activity to contribute ideas to the wall. Do you want more adventure? More time together? More of what you already have? Let everyone add images, paper cuttings, printed visualizations, photos of holidays or moments that made you feel alive. Allow it to inspire you and don't let it overwhelm you with a sense of longing or lack. This wall is your motivation to keep empowering your life to a level where you get to create these experiences more often.

- Raising your home is essential to intentional manifestation. It should be clean and inspired, with space to reflect on your goals. Your home is your "mother ship," your command center, so it must reflect the clarity, passion, and freedom with which you want to resonate, as well as your inner alignment with an external need for comfort, safety, and creativity.

- As you align your home to a high vibration, notice the changes that happen. Use your journal to note the energy that suddenly arises in your life, and how differently you see your ability to take opportunities.

Raise Your Media Awareness

The more you undertake small, potent, sustainable actions, the more universally supported your journey of intentional manifestation will be.

Unless you assess your media habits, however, your manifestations are like attending an exquisite party in your pajamas. You're not ready for the big event; you haven't raised your frequency for an alignment with your future. Preparing yourself energetically means wearing your best mental outfit so that you are psychologically ready to accept your manifestation, and this means making sure your mind is as free from our obsessive media culture as possible.

As a sensitive empath, one of my greatest steps toward making media consumption more bearable was to get rid of the TV. With two children, this was a challenge. But taking that black box off the wall was like getting rid of a vortex that sucked us in and made us vanish from our present moment. Now when we want to watch something, it requires conscious effort, rather than just pushing a button.

Your media diet may make you feel great for a few hours, but does it serve you in a positive way? Evaluate your media consumption by asking yourself these questions:

- What are your media vices—your go-to comforts and habits?

- Are they conscious?

- How do they affect you emotionally and physically?

- Do they bring you joy?

- Are they nourishing?

- Do they teach you anything new?

- Do you use them to escape?

- Are your dreams affected by watching certain movies or TV shows?

When you indulge in dramatic headlines, gossip magazines, or social media, "normal" often becomes a distorted version of reality. Your beautifully unique life often seems a little less satisfying, a little more lacking, and a whole lot more out of alignment. Your vibration can only work with what you give it; if you give it "unattainability," that is exactly what you will get in return.

Here are some more questions that can help you disempower your media habits and enable personal growth at the same time.

- What is it about gossip magazines that you find so fascinating?

- What becomes normalized through television series, films, and social media?

- How do they make you feel in the long run?

- What do they make you think about your life that does not match reality?

You don't have to give up technology to raise your vibration, but you must be aware of what you watch, read, and hear. You can choose alternatives that leave you more satisfied, better nourished, and wiser. There are documentaries about the incredible world you live in, its people, the struggles and triumphs of the human spirit, and informative programs about the mind, body, and soul. There's music that lends perspective on your life, and that can make you feel grateful and inspired. These are high-vibrational emotions that fill you up and motivate you.

When you choose media that raises your emotions to love, ease, and joy, you access an invaluable tool for successful, intentional manifestation. You power yourself with the highest level of consciousness.

Raise Your Emotional Awareness

As you question the elements that feed your media diet, you also need to address the friends and family whose company you keep. If you're like most people, fear of rejection makes you stay attached to people who don't serve the best version of your life. By doing this, you not only dampen the self-empowerment flame you want to nurture, but restrict yourself from truly flourishing.

Surround yourself with people who are humble about their successes, passionate about their self-improvement, and driven by their futures. Sometimes you can politely say no to people who are toxic; at other times you just have to walk away. The more you can sieve out those who disempower your true nature, the more you can raise yourself to a new, higher level of normal.

It's not easy to get rid of these external intravenous systems that have fed your norms and values for decades, but it can create more emotional freedom than most other incremental acts.

Try raising your media awareness and emotional vibrations with the following practices.

Task: *Raise your media and emotional vibrations*

- Incorporate more wholesome, perspective-giving, mind-expanding media in your life. When you sit down to watch your favorite TV series or movie, ask if it will bring value to your life. If you mindlessly click "play" on a social media video, ask if you are really trying to escape your present moment, and if so, why? Question your automatic actions; you will save a lot of time and emotional energy in the long run.

- Use technology to expand your consciousness or motivate you. Learn something every day that will help you achieve your dream. Even one piece of information can be invaluable on your journey.

- Be aware of how many hours a day you spend consuming different types of media. Use a program or app to track your screen time. Be mindful of how much of your day is spent either escaping or expanding.

- Be conscious of what your children watch and how easily they can access media devices.

- Create at least one TV-free day per week. Set aside an afternoon for creative play, or spend time outdoors instead. You can add more of these days as your children get used to the idea of not having the TV on. When you're ready for a complete break, take the TV off the wall and replace it with something truly inspiring; this can create a significant psychological boost for you and your family.

- Be gentle but disciplined about the company you keep. Strengthen your ties with people who inspire you, and release those who do little to encourage the authentic you. Your journey to self-empowerment is hard enough without having to battle those who don't believe in you. Sometimes, to lift your vibration, you must release what's keeping you down.

Intentional manifestation relies on intuitive guidance, a sharp mind, and less influence from low-vibrational emotions. Make sure your "diet" includes a good deal of soul food, spiritual nourishment, and self-empowerment.

Raise Your Body

Your physical diet plays a huge role in your body's ability to tackle stress, hormonal imbalances, and low-vibrational moods. What you put in your body literally becomes the fuel on which your life depends. A high-vibrational food diet supports your body and mind, so they function at their optimal level. I believe that once you have begun to follow a path of conscious living—once you clean and declutter your home, alter your media consumption, and practice freedom of mind—you will naturally be inclined to eat better, cleaner foods because they reflect the level of your alignment.

All food has a vibrational frequency. This is affected by several factors: when it was harvested, whether it was sourced ethically by sustainable means, and how long it took to transport. Fresh, locally sourced, seasonal foods have the highest vibration. Those with added chemicals, monosodium glutamate, high-fructose corn syrup, trans fats, hormones, artificial colors and flavors, preservatives, and artificial sweeteners are on the low-vibrational end of the spectrum. They prevent us from connecting to the vibration at which our higher selves resonate.

If you'd like more information on nutrition, there are many excellent books, like *Low Tox Life* by Alexx Stuart, that can deepen your knowledge about the best foods for your unique energy and body type.

Task: Raise your bodily vibration

If you are trying to clean up your home, mind, and spirit, it goes without saying that you should lift your bodily vibration, too. This is essential to intentional manifestation; your best life includes living in a healthy body that vibrates with holistic wellness and attracts its likeness.

Pay attention to your energy levels and use your journal to note when you are at your lowest during the day. When you feel sluggish, you have no motivation to keep your engines going, no ability to endure through the challenges, and no inner balance with your external world. What food do you turn to when you feel depleted?

What triggers make you overeat, undereat, or turn to unhealthy foods for comfort? Childhood trauma can contribute to eating disorders, and boredom or anxiety can lead to unconscious, destructive eating patterns. When you discover a trigger, notice when it hits and how it affects you. This awareness will help you dismantle its power or seek help, if necessary.

Add natural, unprocessed, unrefined, high-vibrational foods to your diet. Locally sourced, seasonal produce has a low carbon footprint and is usually an economical option. You do not need to shop in a specialized grocery store, spend a lot of money, or learn complicated recipes to consume high-vibrational foods. Choose quality over quantity, and limit meat, dairy products, and alcohol. Regardless of your budget, spending money on your vibrational health is one of the best investments you can make. However, be sure to consult your health care provider before changing your diet.

Some high-vibrational food examples are:

- Fresh, certified organic fruits and vegetables

- Natural supplements like spirulina

- Herbal teas and kombucha

- Pure or filtered water, preferably reverse osmosis or spring water

- Healthy oils like extra-virgin olive oil and cold pressed coconut oil

- Nuts and seeds

- Raw milk dairy products

- Fermented foods like kefir, miso, and tempeh

- Raw chocolate, honey, and maple syrup

- Gluten-free whole grains such as buckwheat, brown rice, quinoa, and amaranth

Just as you should add high-vibrational foods to your diet, there are low-vibration foods you should limit or avoid.

On my personal journey, alcohol was the most difficult of these to drop. It was a symbol of freedom, youth, and nomadic living for me. "Never trust a person who doesn't drink!" was a constant refrain in my family, and as I grew up, I began to drink in competition with my brothers, male friends, and lovers. As anyone who has lived this way knows, it rarely ends well.

I also suffered with crippling depression and anxiety attacks, but I didn't connect these to alcohol until the divine intervention of pregnancy woke me up, pulled me into alignment, and shook me back to life. Now I see the overconsumption of alcohol as detrimental not only to my soul but my life as a mother.

As a South African, meat was also something I consumed nearly unconsciously. Yet there are so many alternative proteins now that eating meat seems almost absurd, especially knowing how harmful meat production can be to the environment. By being more conscious of the meat you feed your family or by eliminating it altogether, and by choosing food that nourishes you over something that makes you feel good in the moment, you can naturally raise your vibration. You may have other associations to something that hurt you deeply, or habits you are not even aware of. Take it one PMS craving, one late-night fast-food pit stop, one Friday night movie at a time.

Low-vibrational food examples:

- Genetically modified foods

- Food treated with chemicals or pesticides

- Processed foods

- Fast food

- White rice

- Bleached flour

- Refined sugar in excess

- Artificial sweeteners

- Coffee in excess

- Soda

- Alcohol in excess

- Mass produced or unethically raised meat, fish, and poultry

- Processed oils like canola oil and cottonseed oil

- Pasteurized cow's milk, yogurt, and cheese

- Deep-fried foods

While you don't actually ingest them, the emollients you put on your skin (makeup, lotions, shampoos, moisturizers) also affect vibrational frequency. (Ironically, you likely think much more about what you put on your babies' or children's skin than you do your own, choosing additive- and perfume-free products for them.) Whatever you put on your skin is absorbed into the epidermis, the layer of dead cells that forms the body's outer layer. While many of these products can help retain moisture or prevent sun damage, they can also cause skin reactions or allergies. Others, depending on their components, are designed to go deeper; some products may even enter the bloodstream. More natural products may be available, so do your research and pay careful attention to ingredients and marketing.

As a woman who once valued her cosmetics bag more than her health, I know what it is like to make this change. It was only when I started to feel more confident in my own skin that I began to consciously lighten up my makeup routine—and my skin thanked me for the freedom. When I made the switch to a high-vibe diet and skincare routine, I no longer had to cover up hormonal acne or create a false glow with makeup—my skin cleared and my moods evened out, allowing me to look in the mirror and feel proud of what I saw.

Changing *how* you see your reflection is always more sustainable than trying to change *what* you see. Appreciating your natural beauty is one of the greatest acts of self-care you can gift yourself.

Raise Your Spending Habits

Becoming more conscious of your spending habits is essential to intentional manifestation. Be aware of the things that fill your life. What energy does this beautiful fabric really hold? What does this plastic toy really contribute? How does the fuel for this car affect a community fifteen thousand miles away?

Raising vibration by changing your spending habits means becoming more aware of your consumer choices. In the last few years, better and more sustainable options for clothing, toys, and consumables have become available. Many use recycled and nontoxic materials; some even help support humanitarian and environmental projects. We have more options now to shop smartly than we have ever had. Start by visiting *www.thecleancollective.com* and educate yourself on a better way of buying your essential home and beauty products.

Imagine, for example, that you find a dress from a high-fashion company online. You don't know how it was produced, who made it, what kind of working environment they had, or what chemicals or toxins it contains. You love the dress, buy it, wear it once, and then it becomes a decoration in your closet for years. The dress cost you money that you go to work every day to earn.

Everything about this story is low-vibrational—except for the emotion you felt when you bought the dress. Consumerism—that addictive feeling of "new"—is said to have the same effect as taking drugs. Unless you address your relationship with consumerism, its interrelated low-vibe effects will start to snowball.

Now imagine another purchase: You need to find a winter jacket. After a few minutes online, you locate a shop that produces the materials used in the jacket with regards to high labor and work standards. When you buy this jacket, the store gives 10 percent of the purchase price to an ocean clean-up project. Although it may have cost you a little more than a high-fashion jacket, you'll save money because you'll buy this only once. You also contribute to more than just the high you get from shopping. High-vibrational consumerism is always minimal, necessary, and aligned with ethical and environmental standards. It's not necessary to use this conscious approach on every new item you buy, but it's important to ask questions about source, quality, and sustainability to raise your vibration and lower your consumer footprint. You can also consider second-hand shops or online sites like Craigslist, which support the pre-loved movement and offer a greater selection of unique items that can reflect your individuality.

By making more thoughtful purchases, you support your manifestations with compassion and gratitude. As you start to see how minimalism is a wealth in itself, you attract more clarity and freedom and develop a mindset that flourishes with kindness and empathy for others.

Task: Raise your vibration through conscious spending

- Write down all the items of clothing, beauty products, accessories, and electronics you want to buy in your future. Take this list with you whenever you go out and use it to consciously buy your items. This stops you from making regretful purchaces, buying the wrong items, or splurging on items you don't need.

Raise Your Language

Your spoken words are vibrations that resonate at a particular frequency. Your inner dialogue has a vibrational resonance, too, and it's often negative:

- "I'm no good at this."

- "I don't look like that."

- "I will never be like them."

These statements shadow your true nature and reflect what you have been made to think is normal, what you believe you can do, and how you are supposed to live. They do not raise your vibration to its highest frequency.

Raising your vibration through self-talk starts by quieting the criticism and listening to the voice of conscious empowerment that says, "Maybe you can." Just as you do yourself no favors by dimming the light of your uniqueness, you do a grave injustice to your intuition by constantly conflicting with it.

Become aware of the message you convey when you talk about yourself. Do you always complain about your job? Your husband? Your in-laws? Lack of money or time? Pay attention so you can see the areas in your life that need attention. Rely on trusted friends to work through these difficulties with you.

Here are some simple tasks to help align your words with a high vibration and give your autopiloted belief system a well-deserved break.

Task: Raise your vibration through language

- We all have that friend or co-worker who talks only about negative things. When you find yourself engaged in such a conversation, stop yourself from responding or change the subject to something positive. This goes for self-talk, too. Gently detach from your negative thoughts and tell yourself as often as possible that getting what you want is just a matter of trust, focus, and intuition. The more you do this, the more you will become these statements. Words have great power when they are consistently repeated into belief.

- When talking about yourself with someone you have never met before, be conscious of your words and their power to shape your reality. Say that you're living the life of your dreams and are who you want to be. "I am" is an incredibly high-vibrational intention that works with the laws of the universe. In making a positive statement about yourself, you put in motion a belief that will literally manifest into your life.

- Be mindful of your words and actions, especially around children— they are little sponges who absorb everything you say and do. The way you speak creates the vibrational vocabulary for the rest of their lives, so slow down, take a breath, and avoid overreacting. Your words are the greatest influence on the way they perceive themselves.

When you start to create more freedom in your mind and begin to live with high-vibrational energy, it will be reflected in your words and actions. You will become the woman who smiles unashamedly at strangers, who radiates energy because she knows exactly who she is and what she wants. You'll be a woman in constant flow, talking with passion about her future, a mover and shaker who always looks like she has freedom and spontaneity in her back pocket. People love her because she makes them feel rejuvenated and lights their souls with inspiration. She holds no insecurities or judgments. She is essentially you, and everyone could do with a little more of her in their daily life.

Raising your self-talk to a higher frequency can also influence your intentional manifestations, because the way you see yourself reflects your confidence, self-empowerment, and ability to navigate your life with certainty.

Raise Your Passions

Hobbies make you feel creative, focused, and inspired. They can give you an idea of your natural talents and passions, and help you access the creativity that makes you truly unique. To raise your vibration by accessing these emotions, you must prioritize your passions and make them a tool for intentional manifestation.

Perhaps you are lucky enough to have a job that incorporates your passions, personal essence, and skills. Or perhaps you have to wait until you're off the clock before you can indulge your creativity. Either way, creativity makes you feel whole, complete, and aligned with your true nature. Here are some tips for making time to raise your vibe and ignite your flame of passion.

Task: Raise your vibration through your passions

Raising your vibration through your passions is a form of soul-care. Although you're juggling important responsibilities, as every mother does, be careful not to neglect your ability to express yourself through your unique talents. Engaging your passions every day brings out the core emotions you want to feel in your best life, attracts more high-vibrational experiences, and solidifies the bond to your higher self.

- Reflect on the elements of your essential nature that have been with you since childhood. Perhaps you were sociable and preferred team activities, or perhaps time alone made you feel most free? What activities did you do then, and why did you stop? A variation of that activity may still suit you, so go back and try things that have always resonated with your passionate self.

- Ask yourself why you do this activity. What makes it feel different from everything else? You may love playing an instrument, for example. You love it because it makes you feel connected to yourself; it requires concentration as well as letting go. It allows you to create spontaneously and express yourself freely. If you share it with others, it may inspire them, too. The more time you give yourself to tap into a passion, the more it will become a part of your ability to express yourself from the core of your being. To know your passion is to know yourself intimately. Be true to yourself and do what lets you express your own quirky uniqueness.

- Plan a personal recess—a few moments in your day that allow you to be creative. If you love doodling, sketching, or drawing, keep a box with your favorite pens and paper handy. Let go of activities that do not serve who you want to be, and fill your free time with activities, people, and emotions that contribute to your vibrational empowerment.

- Consider whether you can objectify your passion.

  - Can you grow it?

  - Is it valuable to others?

  - Does it fulfill a purpose?

  - Are you willing to tend to it at three in the morning after you have been up all night with a sick child?

- If you did it full-time and depended on it as an income, would you still love it?

- If you can answer "yes" to these questions, you are more than ready to start putting a business plan into incremental, achievable goals.

- Tend to your passion and give your spiritual growth time to flourish. Balancing the tension between work, family, and hobby takes time, especially if one has dominated the others for a while. Incremental steps allow for a gentle realignment between the need to survive and the need to thrive, so be patient but persistent.

Raise Your Belief

Belief is the power that creates incredible lives, that accomplishes things no one thought possible, that inspires a world to come together or fall apart. Your self-empowerment journey relies on *how* you believe, not *what* you believe. You can also choose to believe in yourself, your own divine energy, or your power to create your own intentional life.

How do you practice devotion to yourself daily? Do you connect, align, embrace, and let go when necessary? Do you dedicate time to yourself, to your rituals, to study what you believe, to find a like-minded community, to step out of what you know and embrace what you can't sense? Most importantly, do you give yourself time to find guidance? Spirituality is essentially that: the willingness to be guided beyond the mind.

Intentional manifestation requires a belief in something outside yourself because there will always be things that you cannot control. These are the energies working in the universe to shape your life: the job opportunity that comes up, the friendship that springs forth, the partner that suddenly shows up, the child conceived at an exact moment. You have so little control of so much in your life that you should master the few things you can govern, and this starts with belief.

Task: Raise your vibration through belief

- What do you believe in? Have you tried dedicating time and devoting yourself to a practice? Remember, it doesn't matter what you believe in, as long as your belief aligns with who you want to be. Try writing down all your beliefs about yourself, your spirituality, and your connection to something greater than yourself. The more you believe in something—even in the unknown—the greater your manifestation power. Be curious and learn what you need to know to strengthen your connection to your self-empowerment.

- Every time you are told (or tell yourself) that you are not capable of something, remind yourself that you are capable. Replace negative talk with positive affirmations. Sooner than you can imagine, you will no longer have to talk yourself into positivity; it will become your habitual way of thinking. This mindset will change how you see opportunities.

- Reflect on this story about the power of belief:

  Believing in yourself is like standing in a room crammed with thirsty people. In the middle of the room, there are glasses of water, and everyone desperately wants one. You believe that sooner or later someone will come in and hand you a glass. Meanwhile, you wait patiently, your mouth drying up, body withering.

  Suddenly you wonder why you are not helping yourself and why you have to wait for someone to serve you. In that moment you believe that you can serve yourself. You walk up, take a glass, and drink the most exquisite water that ever quenched your thirst. From there, you help others and inspire a community of people to reach their own glasses.

  Belief is the ability to fulfill your greatest intuitive needs first, and then help others fulfill theirs.

- Stop the voice inside your head that says you don't deserve happiness or that is suspicious when things go well. If you're like many people, you often attribute your successes to things that are out of your control, so luck, therefore, must cause happiness. You also tell yourself that good times won't last forever, but you rarely remember this impermanence when things aren't going well. Own your ability to make yourself happy unconditionally.

- Try not to ask others for advice or rely on the internet for answers. Test your intuition by making small, incremental, heart-based decisions. These will build your confidence and enable you to make bigger decisions and changes.

Your beliefs filter into your daily life and create your expectations. In this generation of motherhood, you might believe you should be able to have it all: a happy home, a fulfilling career, time to yourself, and a passionate partner. But you can also live for less stuff and experience more: less habit and more intention; less resistance and more flow; less distraction and more alignment; less holding on and more letting go; less following and more intuition; less separateness and more oneness. These are the beliefs that make your life truly exceptional.

Forgive and thank your past for making you who you are, and then consciously choose what and how you want to believe in the future. Everything is choice, even when your life feels out of control. If you don't believe you deserve your best life, your best body, your best mind, you choose to create resistance to your natural state. By embracing that natural state, you will find it is always filled with limitless potential.

Raise Your Discipline

When you start making disciplined, incremental changes that are aligned with your intuition, you allow goals to manifest from a place of true potency. This is an interdependent process that requires you to sift out low vibrations and focus more on what you love, what feels good, and what creates a sense of true fulfillment.

Sifting takes discipline because you have conditioned yourself to believe that some unconscious habits or beliefs are necessary for your survival. When you know, from a deep and ancient place within, that you need to make changes in your life but never commit to making them, it results in a critical misalignment that causes a "mid-life crisis," crippling anxiety, physical illness, and a life lost to the limitations you've convinced yourself to be real.

Indecision kills opportunity. When you sit on the fence and weigh the scales, you waste valuable time. You scrutinize all possible outcomes, guessing what might happen if you did this or what might go wrong if you did that—even if the only thing you're deliberating is whether to turn up for a coffee date, a new class, or a job interview.

Self-doubt is sneaky. It encourages you to procrastinate until someone or something makes the decision for you. Then you can say, "It wasn't meant to be" or "It wasn't the right time." But now is always the right time to start, do, or learn something that would allow you to make that incremental difference between where you are and where you want to be.

You will always prefer to not change anything because that is where you feel safest. Your mind navigates within your customary spectrum of risk, so when you are deciding whether to change jobs, homes, partners—and you have never made that scale of decision before—your mind will convince you that you need to stay where you are. Problems arise when your intuition conflicts with this conditioned mind, however, because it knows better. Intuition is never indecisive. It never sits on the fence. When you ask it a question, you feel its answer profoundly.

> Do I really want to stay in this job?
> *No, you know it's not good for you!*
>
> Do I really want to wake up feeling this way for the rest of my life?
> *No, you know there is another way!*
>
> Is there something more than this?
> *Yes, absolutely, you know there is!*

So how do you get your ideas out of dead water and your life out of limbo? Discipline.

People who succeed do the things most people don't want to do. They don't give up when it gets tough. They do things differently, they think differently, they take criticism differently, and they don't work until they give themselves a heart attack. They don't binge-watch TV until their minds are numb or eat junk food to get them through the day. They feel their way into decisions quickly and then change whatever is not in alignment. While most of us create quicksand from our disappointments, successful people build stepping-stones with each and every failure. It may sound very masculine to be disciplined, but without the necessary healing powers of feminine energy, you will be disciplining out of alignment.

If you have thought about starting your own business, take this as a personal message from someone who has been there: The only two things you need to make any idea work are discipline and adaptation. First, discipline your mind and convince yourself of your potential for success. Next, adapt as you go. Adapt to new knowledge, changes in technology, cycles of new thought, changes in sociological trends.

I had given myself six months to write a book and find a publisher. Every day I considered the positive effect of completing my goal. Every day I numbed the thoughts that said I couldn't do it and told myself that it was quite possible—until after three months (I recorded the date), I didn't have to convince myself anymore because I believed it to be true. What makes a change takes a change, and I vowed to embrace the art of self-discipline.

I am an advocate for this often-overlooked element of high-vibrational living because I know it works. I was once the polar opposite of who I am today. It was only by disciplining my reactive habits that I turned the biggest corner in my life and manifested into fruition the biggest dream I could imagine. Every time I wanted to run and hide, I told myself to wait and learn.

Making this inner switch gave me everything incredible that I have in my life and it's the most valuable advice I can give you: Discipline yourself to reject what does not feel right; change your ability to face criticism, rejection, and failure; and stop thinking that "comfortable" is "safe." Comfort depends on where you set your thermostat. When you spend enough time living outside your usual temperature range, you can see that comfort is transient and malleable.

Here are a few ways you can raise your vibration by staying disciplined enough to set your manifestations and see them through.

Task: *Raise your vibration through discipline*

- Make sure you are intentionally manifesting what you really want. Align with your higher self through daily meditation and journaling. Remember why you want what you want and how it will benefit others. This will help keep you motivated and make discipline easier.

- Tell yourself you want to be disciplined. If you are like me and previously found discipline difficult, you must first accept that you really want this extraordinary tool that can stop you from reapeating your habitual patterns. Tell yourself that you want to change, that you want to achieve your dream and you want to become the manifestation of your best self. To have a good relationship with discipline, be forgiving and compassionate toward yourself and your conditionings. This feminine approach of "allowing" and forgiving will balance your journey and take the edge off this masculine energy.

- Use your vision board as a gentle motivation to stay on track, focused, and appreciative of where you are right now.

- When you get off track, allow yourself to see the immense benefit that focus can have on your life and celebrate the work behind your actions, not the result itself. Discipline is not about guilt, ridicule, or shame, but about focus and aknowledgement of the little accomplishments.

- You will face hurdles, and that's good! Incredible destinations are not accessed by smooth roads. Turn rejection, criticism, and failure into determination, learning, and allowing. If you fall at a hurdle, get up, assess the situation, see what you can learn from it, and use it as motivation. Never take it personally.

- Know your triggers and make them cues for discipline. Do you want to run when you are criticized? Do you want to eat, cry, or fight when you feel judged? When these emotions are triggered, stop what you are doing and breathe. A moment of conscious awareness will break the reactive pattern and give you the power to make a clearheaded decision on what to do next. Replace the emotion with equanimity or detachment.

- Manage your time. Learn to say "no" instead of saying "yes" reflexively. Add wholesome, nourishing self-care activities to your day; let go of things that weigh you down and don't serve your life as you want it to be. This doesn't mean you won't do your taxes, pay your bills, or wash the dishes in the sink; it means you'll do these necessary activities on a planned schedule, with conscious awareness of the benefit they have to your family.

- Discipline doesn't mean you burn yourself out, but consciously align with your body and mind to know when you are tired, when to take a break, or when to let go. You can only be potently disciplined and efficient when you have the necessary mental and physiological strength. Focus your energy on activities in the morning and be mindful with other activities in the evening. Your 5 a.m. wake-ups will be even more rewarding when you realize they afford you your most productive hours in the day.

- Stop using others to make decisions for you. Take accountability for everything in your life. Whenever you feel like blaming anything circumstantial or anyone personally for their effect on you, stop and see that everything in your life is the result of your conscious or unconscious choices. This is not as horrifying as it may sound; in fact, it's a tool for creating a conscious life based on what kind of future you really want.

- If you are faced with decisions and don't know which way to go, use your heart. If it's the right choice for you, it will feel right, not logical. When you simply can't make a decision, do nothing. Give yourself time and focus on something else in the meantime.

- Showing up is 90 percent of discipline. The more you do it, the more it becomes what you do. So when you take a chance to do something that aligns with your core emotions, show up and learn from it. It will help you grow, expand, and get to know a little more about who you are. One day, you will show up for something or someone that transforms your life—a pivotal lesson or an opportunity. If there's a decision you have to make, something you want to do, commit to it now. Make a plan to achieve it, get up after the hurdles, and keep going.

- Get out of your comfort zone. Allow yourself to experiment with the "unknown," the "impossible," and the "never done before." Many breakthroughs were initially deemed impossible, until someone was determined enough to prove them wrong. Remind yourself that "safe" and "comfortable" will not necessarily lead to your true potential.

Soul-nourishing discipline is the ability to look after yourself and your best interests in accordance with your higher self. It means not letting yourself retread a path that leads to a dead end. Discipline does not punish or shame. It is compassionate toward your conditionings. It focuses on your journey to empower your life and better the lives of others. It allows for spontaneity and the occasional day off.

It is hard work to be constantly aware of who you are, what you are doing, and why you are doing it. You may discipline yourself for a few weeks, perhaps even a month or two, and really give all your attention to your intentional manifestation and high-vibrational living. You eat well, clean up your mind and matter, and create positive mindsets and motivational triggers that allow you to deeply enjoy your life as it is right now, all the while supporting an incredible manifestation into your life. Life feels magnificent; you are steering your own ship for the first time and guiding your life to somewhere you once thought unimaginable.

And then you start to wonder if you can keep it up. You "fall off the wagon" a couple of times, consume too much sensationalized media or junk food, or rekindle a toxic relationship. This time, however, it doesn't feel so good or fill a void like it used to. It feels destructive, unaligned, untrue to who you really are; you suddenly realize that you cannot go back to how life used to be, that you would rather be conscious of every second than be mindless and numb for the rest of your life. Those focused weeks or months of discipline have changed you irreversibly, and your awakening has become the path you walk upon every day. Discipline in the consciousness of your manifestations gives you the power of creation. You no longer live in the realm of limiting beliefs; you are boundless, and suddenly anything is possible.

Part Two

*As you live deeper in the heart,
the mirror gets clearer and cleaner.*

—*Rumi*

PART TWO IS A REFLECTION of how I lived while writing this book. Everything in this section comes from the work I did to realign and redefine my own life to its highest vibration. It really was that moment where everything fell into place and we started to make some bold decisions that we'd delayed for years. I have never been so blessed with opportunity because of it.

I believe we all know deep down what it is that we need to be truly happy, but we have been convinced otherwise by the outside world. Instead of listening to the potency of your inner voice, you have diluted it with low-vibrational media, foods, self-talk, people, and environments. You have been convinced that your voice has no worth because these low-vibrational vices feed on your deepest conditionings, which falsely proclaim that you are not good, strong, confident, masculine, feminine, or smart enough.

I believe that when you become a mother, you reconnect to this intuitive voice. Yet paradoxically, early motherhood is when you are most inclined to seek outside advice and fall prey to others' expectations. A conscious move toward self-empowerment is key as you shape a new generation's norms and values.

When you simmer on a low frequency, toxifying your body and mind with negative media, non-nutritious foods, unconscious consumerism, and negative self-talk, you stay trapped in a state of mindlessness. It takes time to empower yourself, determination to cut away elements that no longer serve you, and self-awareness to see that what you want in life is based on the emotions you want to feel in the future.

As a mother, you must realize that you don't have to sacrifice your dreams to be happy. In fact, your happiness should be a priority because it inspires your family to see the joy that self-care brings: slowing down, looking up, and being present. Self-care may feel paradoxical, but when you notice how much more you can help others after you've taken care of yourself, it becomes a fundamental daily practice. When you are happy and fulfilled, your family is, too. When you are driven by purpose and passion, when you free yourself from your painful past, you emancipate your children.

As you heed your inner voice, you create real freedom for yourself and the generations ahead. Being chained to society's norms and values is like going down with a ship that you don't even captain. Freedom gives you the life vests, emergency boats, knowledge, and power to save yourself.

Aligning your life with your own rules and expectations is the ultimate liberation. It takes commitment and focus to keep to your own path because like everyone else, you are vulnerable to the influences that keep you paddling upstream. But once you see that others' expectations affect your life negatively, it is time to create your own blueprint.

The last section of this book explores the final frontier of self-empowerment: moving beyond the boundaries and limits of your comfort zone so you can continue to carve out a life based on freedom, consciousness, and intent. With freedom as a tool rather than an escape, you will have everything you need to move forward.

FREEDOM OF COMFORT ZONES

CHAPTER 10
Adventure and Wanderlust

Blessed are the curious, for they shall have adventures.

—*Lovelle Drachman*

I SPENT A NUMBER OF years being rather "lost." There was always something that made me an extremist, that made me want to push life to its limits, usually in a destructive and escapist manner. In my late teens I spent time on an island in the South Pacific. I loved it—the ease of life, the humidity, the constant sound of the shushing ocean, and the people. I felt a spiritual belonging in its beautiful culture.

Life on the island changed me forever. I cannot hear the rhythmic beat of a slit drum or even open a jar of coconut oil without old memories surfacing. It sometimes calls me back, the simplicity and slowness of it all, the separation from the rest of the world.

I eventually left to go to university, but I could not wait to hear the island's heartbeat again. As soon as my studies were over five years later, I packed up and went back. The little village looked just the same. Such little development had happened in those five years that I was able to recognize the same people in the same places as if I had never left. The village itself was locked in a time warp from the 1950s, with cruising Cadillacs and hand-stenciled signposts. Time was static; I never quite knew what day, month, or year it was. Everyone lived on "island time," where no one was ever really early or late for anything.

On my return visit, I felt the same connection that I had before, but something had changed in me. After almost a year of timeless living, my watercolor dreams began to granulate into pixels, the air thickened, and the lack of change suffocated me. It was a moment in my life where I felt my heart break without a persecutor being present.

My dream of island life slowly but persistently turned into a nightmare. I started to miss the things I had never truly appreciated—the coolness of European air, the richness of city cultures, the cycles of nature, and ultimately, the challenges of real life. I left six months later.

I have since made peace with those adventures, knowing that there were many lives I could have stepped into, but that none resonated as fully as the one I have right now. Motherhood was my initiation into true personal growth, not just because I could no longer escape, but because for the first time, I didn't want to leave something behind.

Running *toward* something is not the same as escaping *from* something. I still travel extensively (with my family), I still run (for the exercise), and I still feel like an extremist, in the sense that I go against the grain to create my own version of life.

It is a rebellious act to decide for yourself how you want to live, work, and play. I encourage you to liberate yourself by embracing contrast, adapting, and reaching beyond your comfort zone. What you learn will truly develop you as an individual. Change is an instigator of conscious expansion and without it, there is little real fulfillment in life.

Through the practices that inspired this book, my perception of adventure changed significantly. My heart beat more rapidly on my son's first day of school than it did during my Nevis bungee jump in New Zealand. I have explored more of our neighborhood than I ever would have before having children. This new appreciation for adventure has enhanced my desire to explore this beautiful planet in a new way, and as a family. It was a gift I never expected in becoming a mother—the ability to truly see the world and to embrace my sudden sense of responsibility for its survival.

I now prioritize experiences, adventures, and high-vibrational living. We traded our big family house for a small communal apartment and decorated it with our photos of swimming in oceans, surfing, exploring castles, watching sunsets, hiking, finding creatures, waking up in campervans, and sipping coffee at sunrise—creating a lifelong investment bank of memories for all of us.

We are most proud of the trips that took us only a few kilometers away—camping in an open bungalow, pitching our tent at a local festival, or making a bonfire at the beach and roasting marshmallows on the shores of the Kattegat. These adventures mean the most to us and give us the greatest sense of freedom because they don't involve expenses, flights, or extensive planning.

While I miss my easy, pre-baby access to adventure and the thrill of the unknown, my slower pace lets me really notice the adventure that is all around us. As a family that lives with intention, our everyday adventures come in the form of taking an alternative route to school or having a *Fredag slik* ("Friday sweet"—a traditional weekly treat for kids in Denmark) on a Monday. These little acts of rebellion teach our children that while rules keep you safe, you can also define terms and conditions for fun.

§ ℭ℟

Part Three is an inspirational guide to stretching your comfort zone beyond its usual boundaries. It's not going to tell you to pack up your bags, spend all your money, or put your family on hold while you sit in an Indian ashram for a year, but it will encourage you to break the normality of your confining comforts. It's about changing the thermostat, allowing some time to flourish outside of your usual temperatures, and accommodating spontaneity, which is too often lost in motherhood.

This section outlines three final steps that will guide you into an expansive life. They will not only help you embrace the power of change but encourage you to grow in ways you never believed possible. By the end of the last chapter, you will know how to answer that question that keeps you up at night—the one that tethers you to that repetitive dream, the one that just won't let you settle for what is. We all have that question, and your life is about to expand beyond its boundaries as you answer it.

Stay aligned, stay true to your conscious self, and take a bold leap that will lead you into the unknown. Too often we wait for tragedy or unbearable suffering to make the changes we need. But I believe it is better to change under the conscious conditions of love and joy.

Expand Your Comfort Zone

Your comfort zone is a behavioral space that confines your thoughts and actions to a routine pattern, which minimizes anxiety, stress, and risk. It gives you mental security, since it is easier to stay where you feel safe than to face the unknown. The less you embrace change, however, the more you create a stagnant life where professional opportunities, life experiences, and spiritual growth cannot flourish.

Like everyone else, you have been conditioned to seek predictability; in fact, most of what you do habitually is unconscious. You wake up, go through the same routine, and work with the same people in the same environment. This "predictable unawareness" creates an enormous obstacle to change.

Be aware of the excuses and habits that make you feel like you're in control when you're really just following reactive patterns. Step outside of your comfort zone and counter your unconscious autopilot. Train your emotions to stop repeating the same, predictable manifestations. Shaking things up means doing things differently:

- Go for a walk when you want to eat

- Read a book when you want to watch TV

- Say no when you would usually say yes

- Take another route to work

- Write in your journal instead of stewing in your negative thoughts

- Learn from your failures instead of running from them

- Stop making excuses and choose to be accountable

- Be compassionate instead of critical

- Use meditation instead of anger

- Be illogical and off-schedule

You probably have "comfort statements" that define the parameters of what you are willing to risk:

- "I don't do camping. It's too outdoorsy."

- "I will never run for the fun of it. It's just not in my nature."

- "I'm not the kind of person who can be spontaneous. I need to plan."

But comfort zones are created from fear. You don't know what will happen if you take that step into the unknown. Maybe you've have had a bad experience, so you play it safe, because safe is what you know. Routine is comfortable, and everything settles into routine when we repeat it for a long enough time. In essence, comfort zones are just acquired routines that were themselves once unfamiliar. Remember that new job you took? That new place you moved into? That baby you had? They are part of your life now. Anyone who has had a baby knows the difference twenty-four hours can make. Even a dramatic change can be followed by adaptation and result in comfort again.

It takes practice to reach beyond the veil of comfort, but it has led many a great person to an extraordinary life. To reach beyond your comfort zone is to step onto the path of abundant opportunity; all you have to do is let go of your resistance to change. This will begin your evolution from surviving to thriving.

Task: Expand your comfort zone

- Teach your unconscious, habitual emotions that your conscious mind is in charge by meditating every day for at least ten minutes. The more you train your mind to sit quietly in a state with few sensual triggers, the more you can decide on which emotions you want to fuel your life. When practiced consistently, you will start to create a new pattern of emotions that taps into the best version of your life. This will bring you more opportunities, more valuable lessons, and more moments of pure joy every day.

- Use your vision board. As suggested in Parts One and Two, this is a tool to help you determine the core emotions you want to experience in life, instead of letting your habitual, reactive emotions spin you on the same manifestation merry-go-round. Add images that inspire and motivate you. Define yourself with images of the future you envision, and you will be free of the predictable past.

- Take your goals on holiday. Ever wondered why you feel so relaxed and free on vacation? It's because you're out of your usual environment. Your home and work environment simply reaffirm who you think you are and what you think you can do, so get out, get away, and let inspiration come to you. Take your journal, your digital visual board, and your meditation mat wherever you go; spend a few moments every day seeking perspective on your habitual life. A new environment might lead you to a personal breakthrough, a valuable realization, or a spontaneous business idea that never had the chance to get through your resistance before.

- Journal about a time when you were pushed (or pushed yourself) out of a comfort zone. What happened? You will probably find that the situation resulted in some kind of personal growth, and if it didn't, perhaps there was a lesson to be learned.

- What situations push you out of your comfort zone? Write down the triggers (fears and environments that make you feel uncomfortable) and your reactions. For example, if you hate public speaking, you might react with anxiety, fear, and dread when asked to make a speech. Once you know this, shift to a conscious reaction—don't be fooled by the limits you have set for so long. Tell yourself you love this idea, you are excited about it, and it's going to be great. It might seem odd at first, but if you do this every time, you'll change your predictable pattern and adopt a new blueprint. You may start to love public speaking, camping, or taking the spider out of the bathtub. What starts as pretending literally turns into a new normal.

- Get over difficult experiences quickly. When you dwell on a negative event, it starts to determine your mood, your state of mind, and even your general disposition. From now on, let go of what you can. Practice detachment, equanimity, and compassion toward the situation; don't let it become embedded in your core. The more flow you can bring into your experiences, the more control you will have over the emotions you experience in the future.

Much of your life is dictated by your unconscious reactions and comfort zones. These are erected to minimize risk and avoid previous painful experiences, but eventually they define who you are, where you go, what you do, and how you express yourself. It's time to grow beyond your pruned flowerbed into a vast meadow of wildflowers.

Expand Your Wanderlust

Take a minute to do a quick internet search on the social media hashtag "#wanderlust." You'll see posts by escapists, dreamers, and seasoned travelers enjoying the world's most amazing places. The posts capture the world's beauty, but they also suggest that only incredibly lucky people get to do these amazing things. Very rarely do you see a picture of a mother.

At this point in my life, I can only imagine what it would be like to take a glamorous selfie on a tropical mountainside—one arm outstretched to hold the camera, the other reaching back to grasp my husband's hand. In reality, it'd be too hot for my two-year-old daughter to walk so I'd be carrying her sweaty, chubby body, while my son pulled me toward something he found more interesting, and my husband would have been too distracted to realize that we'd forgotten the water bottle. I can see why images like this don't top the #wanderlust rankings.

I believe wanderlust is one of the most important "lusts" you can have. How can you teach your children to treasure the Earth and its awesome beauty if they have never experienced it for themselves? Although I traveled extensively before I became a mother, I have never felt more lust to wander than I do now—because I can't wait to show my children that the world does not stop at the end of our road.

Being pragmatic about the demands of both motherhood and travel, I started small. I don't believe you need to spend lots of money, travel for hours, or even leave the neighborhood to satisfy your curiosity about the world. In fact, my definition of "wanderlust" includes the desire to explore the nooks and crevices of our own neighborhood, discover the incredible vastness of our own mental landscapes, and uncover the beauty that lies within and all around us.

When you're curious about where you live, you don't need to save up to take that trip to Thailand, Borneo, or Bali; instead, you can discover something new and genuinely inspiring every day. To some, especially those who traveled before having children, going to the local park will never equal a trip to South America. I understand that very well. However, if you suggest that one environment is better than another, you teach your children that only certain places and situations can make you happy. The fact is that everything just is, and becoming unconditional in your happiness means that you can experience joy no matter where you are in the world.

Exploring our local area with my kids teaches them to explore the larger world with the same set of curious eyes. They feel the same excitement packing their bags for a trip to our cabin as they do when packing for a trip to Australia. They'll learn more from a weekend camping in the local woods than they will from a weekend in their apartment. They're just as bored on the plane for thirty-five hours as they are in the car for two hours. You can expect your children to dislike travel when you're stressed about it. As a parent, you now have a new and daunting responsibility in your travels: You have to create a level of excitement and curiosity within yourself so that everyone can have more fun.

Here are some ideas to inspire your wanderlust.

Task: Expand your wanderlust

- Subscribe to magazines that inspire your family to travel. When you choose a destination, allow yourself to discover something new. You may believe you will relax better on an all-inclusive holiday, but those are rarely the trips that your children remember. You can choose to return to work unfulfilled by two weeks on a sun lounger or rejuvenated from a fortnight of bonding, sharing, and filling your memory box with genuine adventures.

- Sign up for local newspapers and discover events that are going on right under your nose. Once a month, let your family pick a new event.

- Clean up your social media feed so that you only follow genuinely inspirational, relatable, and encouraging accounts that share family wanderlust stories. Their posts should inspire you to travel—not make you feel that they are doing something you can't. There are some incredible sites that depict both parenthood and adventure.

- Learn about an environmental issue. Research an element you love, like the ocean or the forest, and educate yourself and your children about this issue. Many government and university websites focus on the environment. Another good option is to have a National Geographic family night, where each family member writes down an element (Water, Earth, Air, Fire) or an animal and puts their preference into a hat. One person chooses one note from the hat and everyone watches an episode from the National Geographic on that subject.

- Buy a travel guide for somewhere you have always wanted to go, even if you have not planned a trip yet—we've inspired many of our family holidays this way. When I have information on a place, city, or country, I feel much braver. Knowledge is confidence when it comes to family travel, so empower yourself.

- Update your vision board with images of places you would like to go and encourage your children to contribute their ideas and dreams. Have a family meeting and discuss places they have heard about at school or from friends. Start planning a trip by posting information, travel guides, tips, and accommodation ideas.

- If you can't travel this year, ask yourself what local spot you'd like to explore. Have you heard of a place close by that you've never visited before? You might find yourself amazed at how little you know about your city or country; exploration will connect you to it in a much deeper way.

As a self-confessed free spirit and wanderlust-driven woman, travel has become something of a paradox for me. No one talks about wanting to spend time on their own when they become a mother, or says they need time alone for introspection and personal growth. Self-care has been packaged as the idea that a ten-minute DIY banana face mask will set you right again.

Being conscious of your "extremist" needs is to know yourself as a whole. Whatever your wanderlust, your being-alone dream, your singular escape— embrace it, and listen to what it is trying to tell you. Perhaps it misses you, perhaps it just wants to talk, and perhaps it doesn't like being ignored because it makes you who *you* are. Find a way to integrate it into your life. After all, motherhood means coming into alignment with both roots and wings; we must balance them to find true freedom.

Expand Your Adventure

Even though I have traveled extensively, I would not call myself a true adventurer and identify more with the word "escapist". Risk was always relative—I never had much invested in anything, so it was easy to make big decisions. I remember being told stories of my adventurous, seafaring ancestors who rode the maritime tea clipper route between the United Kingdom and Sri Lanka, racing other ships to deliver their cargo.

My family history is filled with incredible stories like that: escaping Europe to settle in Africa during World War II, and surviving a shipwreck in Japanese waters during World War I. Most recently, an aunt educated at Oxford University gave up a highly paid corporate job in Sydney to live on a small island in the Pacific. (This is what adventure and uncharted territory look like nowadays—stepping off the treadmill and doing what you want, not what is expected of you.)

The inherited trauma of those survival experiences, however, conditioned me to stay within my comfort zone. You, too, want your children to bypass experiences that create suffering, so you spend a lot of energy living in and teaching avoidance. But you have an innate need for adventure—because life itself is a journey of discovery. Adventure can be found in everything when you choose to be curious about life. Curiosity fueled the expansion of human knowledge, so the less inquisitive you are, the less you know and grow as an individual.

One day at my daughter's daycare I noticed a mother and her child taking part in an animated discussion about their recent holiday: "Remember when we climbed that mountain?" and "Tell them about the trip to the waterfall!" I was intrigued and just about to join the conversation when suddenly the mother saw her daughter rolling around and playing on the floor. She became noticeably distressed and picked the child up, exclaiming that she was touching all kinds of germs, dirt, and bacteria. (The floor looked clean by my standards.) What a conflict between words and actions! This woman was clearly adventurous enough to climb mountains and bask in the beauty of waterfalls, but she couldn't let her child roll around on the floor like a regular two-year-old. If you go on exotic holidays to seek adventure but limit yourself in everyday curiosity, then perhaps the money would be better spent on books and not experiences.

As I reflected on the limits of my own comfort zone, I noticed a pattern. As soon as I became a mother, I became uncomfortable with uncertainty and a lack of routine. Thus, I began to restrict my travel to places I knew or had thoroughly researched, making sure I could predict as much of the outcome as possible. I made sure I was in control of where and when we went and always had an exit plan. After a couple of years of living without adventure, I realized this was inhibiting my fulfillment both as a mother and as a person. I even began to fear a once-fundamental part of my life: explorative travel. My comfort zone no longer served who I really was.

We had a few weeks of parental leave left from our first child and I was six months pregnant with my second when we took the trip of a lifetime. I dreamed of traveling across a foreign country in a camper van, sleeping under the stars and by the ocean, getting as lost as we possibly could, without a map and without a schedule. So we booked a van and set off on a trip around Portugal, armed with nothing more than a surfboard and a pregnancy pillow. It played on every comfort zone and pushed every boundary I had.

Thankfully, I was in the company of an incredibly robust three-year-old and ex-army officer husband, who helped out in more than a handful of hairy situations. When our van broke down in the middle of the mountains halfway through the trip, I used the last power bar on my phone to call the first campsite I could find. We landed in a place that we have since gone back to numerous times. That trip played a massive part in our ability to take risks because it taught us that we can face anything. It brought us together in a way that touched me forever—living so close, experiencing so much, and needing so little.

When you are grounded by strong, dependable foundations like a supportive family, you can take risks without fearing that they will break you. My husband and I have also indulged our individual wanderlust and taken trips on our own. By allowing each of us to have our own space, these solo adventures have benefitted us enormously both as a couple and as a family.

Adventure is a practiced skill, and it takes time to overcome years of habits that make you want to give up when things get uncomfortable. Push yourself to do something that feels unfamiliar. The more you practice this, the more rewarding the adventure becomes. The feeling of discomfort becomes an incredible trigger for you to learn a little more about yourself through the experience.

Here's how you can include more adventure, curiosity, and transformative experiences in your life.

Make it personal

- Identify your individual wanderlust in your journal. What do you want to do on your own? Listen to the voice that asks for solitude. Allow yourself to prioritize it in whatever way will benefit you most. A weekend away once a year, a class once a week, a creative outlet once a day?

- In your journal, list all the thrilling things you've done or amazing places you've visited. Take a moment to remember the freedom you felt and the untethered wonder you might have experienced, even if it was something relatively simple. By doing this, you acknowledge that adventure is within you, and igniting those high-vibrational emotions can make life a truly remarkable journey.

- In your journal, write about the last time you felt the thrill of adventure. Where were you? What were you doing? What was it that made you feel these emotions? What made you feel adventurous? Perhaps you were on holiday and you tried a new food for the first time. Or you felt adventurous because the new environment made you feel like you didn't have to be your predictable self.

- Now ask yourself how you could be more adventurous in your everyday life. Could you try new foods or take a new class? Spend time in a new environment that frees you to be a more unusual you? Make it a priority to find places and experiences that resonate with your adventurous self. And the next time you take a trip to the park, spend five minutes on a swing. It might literally push you out of your comfort zone to look a bit silly, but the benefits of feeling your heart roll over will be enough to reignite your desire for exhilaration.

- Think about how the word "adventure" fits into your current life. Does it sound like something from a foreign language? Or perhaps like it belongs to someone younger and freer? Adventure is your personal ability to push beyond the predictable. It's doing something different. It's momentarily stepping away from yourself to embrace little, fearless acts that challenge you. If you feel like taking a different route to work, that is an adventure. If you try camping even if you're not sure you'll like it, that is an adventure. If you usually take skim milk in your coffee but decide to order a full-fat one with trimmings—that is an adventure. Before you know it, little acts of adventure turn into bigger decisions that lead to the greatest expanse of all: the one within.

Make it local

- When incorporating more adventure into your daily life, start with where you live. Plan accessible trips that require little travel time and preparation. You can visit a new park or plan a weekend day to simply "get lost." Even routines can hold adventure when you approach them with curious eyes. Take a magnifying glass on your adventures with the kids and explore the things you find. Climb the highest point you can and take in some perspective.

- Find a local wilderness spot that has camping grounds. Areas where you can build a campfire and explore nature provide the best experiences for younger children.

Make it free

You hardly want to invest in something totally new and adventurous only to find that you (or the family) were not in the best mood to experience it. The cost of such an experiment might create a negative experience that will inhibit your doing it again. When starting out, keep it free, fun, and frivolous. Attend museums on free-entrance days and subscribe to information about free local events. Pack a lunch and snacks to keep everyone's vibrations high. The more free adventures you can pack into your week, the more you can shift into a mindset that accommodates openness and the possibility of bigger investments.

Make it a holiday

Plan an alternative family holiday. Try a week of surfing or a family yoga retreat. As much as an all-inclusive beach holiday provides relaxation, it rarely offers the chance to experience wonder. Nature holidays with older children provide tech-free experiences that truly bring families closer. Off-grid retreats, "glamping" sites, cabins in the forest, yurts, tree houses … there are many types of accommodations that will show you new forms of relaxation.

These holidays will give you much more revitalized energy than the ones that sedate you with all-day booze and buffets. If choosing to be with your kids instead of getting a babysitter sounds like more of a chore than a holiday, invite extended family, grandparents, or other tribe members on your trip. Not only will you have extra hands to ensure some personal time, but you'll get to experience life-transforming adventures with those you love. Children will always remember experiences over things, and alternative holidays provide fundamental grounding and perspective that they will rely on later in life.

Make it solo

If you can't regenerate yourself at home on a daily basis, the emotional and physical distance provided by solo travel can be life-changing. I have known many a dedicated mother who makes solo travel a yearly priority; by allowing your partner to do the same, you encourage trust, love, and mutual freedom that will be returned in the most fulfilling way. Talking with your partner or spouse about more personal time away is the first step to solo adventure, and knowing it is reciprocal can become cathartic.

Make it relative

If you are like me and often dream of exotic locations, I have an insight that might help you. The "hedonic adaptation" theory states that while your happiness level fluctuates with circumstances, it naturally reverts to a set point. Your genetics determine about 60 percent of this set point, but external factors can still influence a significant 40 percent—for better or worse.

If you never make time for yourself, can't deal with stress, disregard the small things, and see yourself as a victim, then it will be very difficult to increase your happiness by moving to a tropical country, getting a new car, or even winning the lottery, because after a while, you will revert to your set point of contentment.

Once you make the effort to change your mindset, however, you will not only better your life now, but you will lock in that positivity for the future. Hedonic adaptation and the law of attraction are best friends in this regard, so if you intentionally manifest a goal, make sure to work on your practices of gratitude and mindful awareness in everyday life.

Make it rational

Adventure is a natural part of children's lives, but as they grow it gets compartmentalized into "risks," "fears," and "dangers." Teach your children to respect risks and dangers, but help them distinguish between rational and irrational fears. Although fear is a psychological tool that can keep you safe, it plays no positive part in emotional well-being. This is a great step forward in embracing the unknown.

SUMMARY

Part Three

A person susceptible to wanderlust is not so much addicted
to movement as committed to transformation.

—*Pico Iyer*

As a member of this generation, you are no longer confined to the town and culture in which you were born. With a free mind of acceptance and compassion, you can become a true adventurer who dares to experience the unknown. However mundane your routine, it is a fundamental part of your grounding, a supportive structure that allows you to take risks. But an imbalance between your inner and outer worlds can create a struggle for equilibrium. Adventure, however, can balance your roots with wings.

When you push through and beyond your comfort zone, you are no longer tied to reactive patterns. As you become a little braver, a little more detached from the conditionings of your past, you'll notice your ability to incorporate adventure into your everyday life. Soon, you won't be satisfied with your usual way of doing things and you'll indulge in little acts of rebellion that make you feel truly alive. Perhaps a different route to work today. Perhaps a plan for the weekend up by the lake. Perhaps a holiday to a place you've never been, doing something you've never done.

Soon you'll start to realize that all of life is an adventure and everything is meant to be discovered. You'll get "the bug." Once the wanderlust for your own life takes over, you will see how enslaved you have been to your comfort zone. You'll realize that you have freedom because you can choose to see things differently, to untether yourself from the things that no longer serve you, and to create the future you want to live.

You'll flourish. You'll be able to regard change without fear and vibrate at a frequency of the highest resonance, manifesting anything you dream up. Your simple task of incorporating more adventure into your life will become a soul-nourishing illumination for the rest of your days. You will learn that openness, consciousness, and freedom lead to transformation more quickly than any force you have ever tried before.

Life beyond the Book

WHEN I FIRST SENT THIS book out to publishers, I received many colorful replies. One said: "As I read this book, I kept thinking, 'Why doesn't she just settle?!' I got so frustrated that you could not just settle down and stop worrying about all this freedom nonsense."

To me, this letter personified people with limited perspectives, those who dishearteningly believe that they cannot create their own destinies.

I wrote this book for people like you, people who still believe freedom is there for the taking, people who know that they can create their own life by design and intent. I wrote this book for people who won't sit when they are told to, who won't just get on with it, and who refuse to settle down.

That is why I decided to keep traveling when I became a mother. It is my act of rebellion, a beacon for those who have unknowingly settled, who are stuck in a life they do not truly enjoy. It's an act of defiance to those who gasp at the idea of flying thirty-seven hours in economy with two kids under four years old. A little revolution for those who believe a woman should be tamed by marriage and caged in domesticity. A tiptoe insurrection for those who commute every day to a box that confines and defines them, or who live in an environment that they know is sterile.

While I have always believed I was destined for an extraordinary life, I too got lost. When I became a mother, I felt I had to be a certain way. I was herded into silent expectations and rules of behavior. My life became unconscious. Eventually, I broke. But putting the pieces back together made me determined to let go of anything that no longer served me. It was a constant process of creating, breaking, and healing, as it will be for you on your journey.

I hope that your journey through this book has shown you that freedom is consciousness. Your awareness of your thoughts, emotions, and habits are the first step toward gaining control of your life. Inner freedom means detachment from anything that ties you to a one-size-fits-all existence; it is essentially unconditional. Freedom is flow, openness, and intention. By tapping into the vibrations that create worlds, you rise to your natural state of higher connection.

Manifestation of the best version of your life starts today. Will you define yourself with an intentional future or the predictable, habitual, and unconscious past?

You can start right now with small incremental changes to your reactive thoughts. It may take a few months to realign yourself with freedom, but it will take less time than trying to force change on an unconscious life. When you have freed your mind from its limiting conditions, the rest will fall into this beautiful space of flow and opportunity.

You can expect challenges when others discourage or judge you. It can be a lonely walk through your inner midnight. You may feel like you are a deserted wanderer, the only one traveling in this direction, but you are never alone. We are here with you—the other readers of this book, the ones who smile at you on the street, the friends who want to talk about deeper, more spiritual topics, the ones who compassionately help you, and the ones who love you without expecting anything in return.

Be persistent with your inner alignment, and you will create a life that holds every moment in joy and ease. Release your resistance and you will flow abundantly through life. Learn what you can so you can get where you need to go. Never forget that every situation holds a lesson; these become the stones that pave the way across future hardships, not only for yourself but for your children, too.

We are all in this together. We all come from different walks, but we are all connected to the freedom that flows between the solid stones of life. Smile at someone, be kind, give back, be bold and unashamed of who you really are and what you really love to do. Dream big, be humble, and live with wanderlust for your own life.

Your world is a reflection of yourself. You are wild and ancient, scientific and spiritual, masculine and feminine. You are an empowered being with all the resources you could ever need to live an abundant life. Start living like it is already yours and it will come intentionally, boldly, unexpectedly, easily.

Take your children with you. The world needs more rebellious, conscious families who inspire original ideas and share their curiosities. Be careful with what you teach your children; inspire them by living your own conscious life. Show them that to be human is to be free, present, and compassionate. Tell them that everyone has the right to choose the life they want; show them how to do it by living in accordance with your own rules. Be the inspiration that you wish for them. Live the life you want for them. Don't spend your days working to give them the opportunities you never had—be present and show them that opportunity comes from being open to the world. Pave the road that leads them to their own creativity.

If the secret to happiness is freedom, the secret to freedom is courage. Fail well, with humility, and pick yourself up with determination. Use failure as a chance to learn or let go, then continue the journey to discovering the best version of your life. Never accept the cultural collective as a rule for your own life. Spend more time doing what makes you truly happy than living in the lack of what doesn't. Conscious creation takes time and adjusting, slow brewing through expansive experiences.

Lastly, remember to keep your own definition of wanderlust in your life. It could be something that makes you unique—a dream, a personal longing, a bit of space to simply be. Self-nourishment is best kept alive through passion, so do something that makes you feel truly "you" often. It is not only the secret act of incredible mothers, but of all free women.

A B O U T   T H E
Author

SEZ IS AN ACCLAIMED POETESS and creative writer, born in South Africa to a family from six different cultures. She has traveled extensively and lived in some of the most remote parts of the world, including many years spent in Sri Lanka deepening her spiritual practice. After two children, Sez settled into a more conventional life and became a creative writer for some of the biggest fashion brands in Europe. After years of struggling with anxiety and chronic depression due to the societal pressures of being a mother and working full-time, Sez redesigned and downsized her entire life to fit the freedom and wanderlust she once resonated so deeply with. Sez now lives in a commune in Denmark with her Viking husband and children, and she continues to travel adventurously throughout the world with her young family. Sez empowers people with transformational mind, body, and soul guides that inspire her readers to live truly unique, unconventional, and untethered lives, driven by their own blueprint of freedom. Sez will awaken you to your own free-spirited nature, which has the power to guide you to your own truly authentic, abundant, and deeply nourishing life.

CONNECT WITH
Sez

Sign up for Sez's newsletter at
www.sezkristiansen.com/soulfriends

To find out more information visit her website:
www.sezkristiansen.com

Facebook Page:
www.facebook.com/sezkristiansenauthor

Instagram
www.instagram.com/sezkristiansen

Check out her other book on Amazon
Healing HER by Sez Kristiansen

BOOK DISCOUNTS

& SPECIAL DEALS

ONE LAST THING...

Thank you for reading! If you found this book useful, I'd be very grateful if you'd post a short review on Amazon. I read every comment personally and am always learning how to make this book even better. Your support really does make a difference.

Search for *Inspired Mama* by Sez Kristiansen to leave your review.

Thanks again for your support!